Down Town

True tales of trial and triumph on the mean streets

ROBERT E. LIPSCOMB

Eagle's View Press, LLC.
ST. LOUIS

ISBN 0-9661926-1-3

First published in 2006 by Eagle's View Press, LLC.

Printed in the United States of America
Set in Palatino Linotype

Soli Dei Gloria

"And he who would save his life, must first lose it…"
Luke 17:33

"To escape, escape from this, this unsatisfactoriness…"
Buddha

"So I went into the wilderness because I wished to live deliberately, to front only the essential facts of life and see what I might learn from what it had to teach."
Henry David Thoreau

Preface

It has been over five years since I first left the middle-class life behind and set out onto the streets of a struggling city, to be homeless, broke, alone. While everything has changed since that time, and only now have I found the courage to set it all down for others to see, it remains a deeply set part of who I am and, I believe, a useful story. Usefulness is so important to me personally, to the real world, to anyone who might chose to invest a few dollars and the time to read this, I determined from the outset to craft this work as a tool, a reference piece, in part, a morality tale. I do not insist that my reality is alone true or cannot be paralleled. Of the estimated nine dimensions, perhaps mine is just one. Do I even know it well enough to tell it?

The majority of this book was written over a period of two years, usually at the middle table in the Fine Arts section of the St. Louis Public Library Central. I have done due diligence to capture, inter-rogate, torture out the truth of the matters at hand, to tame the creative beast. My mind has oft been likened to video games, a psychologically-based psp with cheats and traps, treasures and weapons, tools and gateways. I have throughout attempted not so much to create some written work but rather to create my self. To elude and transcend, if not quite escape, even in the midst of exile. Occasionally, I have employed celebration to maintain my wits, as I believe wit is a shimmering shadow of the Holy Spirit, an innate internal resolution to dissipate the absurdity of it all. I do not believe I have actually despaired, having supped at the table of Mammon's Eucharistic existential ennui to gluttony. How could I be satiated by mere, common despair?

I have been sufficiently fortunate for the majority of my life, at least, in terms of material things. Once upon a time, I was a young soldier in an extraordinarily unpopular Army. I have owned and operated small businesses and profited thereby. My first wife bore me a magnificent boy-child, blond and blue-eyed who now is married and pursuing his own life story. My second wife was nearly a generation my junior, a buxom blonde beauty who had recurring roles on TV shows and in the Oscar-winning movie *The Fugitive* and, also, *Groundhog Day* with Bill Murray, (a super fellow*), Leave It to Beaver* and, that sports movie which has become a classic of the genre, *Rudy*. That lasted all of about a year-and-a-half. The same arrogance and belief that I could be whatever I wanted to be under any circumstances is not a new phenomenon. I have never had to carry the cross of either drug or alcohol addiction. In short, I have damn few excuses for anything that went awry.

Throughout most of it, my primary mission in life seemed to be to ruthlessly pursue the next, great distraction, piling momentary diversion one upon another. It made for some sorry contours in life. Superfluous, amorphous, existing without real authenticity, I came to realize that old Bob had to be assassinated with certain cold rage. Thus, I left it all behind, piece by piece, in the attempt to cleanse myself of the sin of existence.

Ah, but that's just the tip of the iceberg. The rest of the story and what to make of it all I must leave to the good reader. I have learned along the way that trying to explain one's self is usually a futile gesture, much less attempting to explain one's art.

I feel I must, however, at least give you the gist of how this particular book came to be. I blame it squarely on my former English teachers and a bunch of pretty girls. That's right, if there was a cutie I was interested in, I'd write her term paper or book report, invariably gaining a better grade for that work than one signed by yours truly. (Teachers' pets and that sort of thing, one must suppose…) I have used the craft of writing for personal gain and therapy ever since. Thus it was that, once embarked on the adventure before me, I turned, as always, to that certain solace, placing ink on paper.

Which creates its own problems if one is without the funds to buy pens or paper. So I ventured into a warm-enough, downtown church and begged some writing stuff from the first secretary I could find. Her name was Carol Bledsoe and therein lays another tale, which you will encounter in this book, also.

Over time, a young, bright social entrepreneur named Jay Swoboda met up with me and together we began producing a street magazine named *Whats Up*. Most of what I wrote for him never saw the light of day and, I suspect, for good reason at the time. I also penned a short piece about living on the street for the Episcopal newspaper *Interim*. It began to slowly dawn on me that my words had effect, that I could probably make a decent living doing this. Someday. Then, I entered a writing contest and, despite hundreds of other fine pieces submitted, won. That award was in the nonfiction category for NASNA in 2003.

All along the way, many have encouraged me to re-gather my original writings and to add additional reflections about what turned out to be an incredible journey of faith and friendships, culminating in a fairly dramatic personal triumph in the face of much adversity. It has required this book to hold forth all the tales of trial and triumph on the mean streets. I hope you enjoy it as much as I have enjoyed writing it.

One final note may be in order here. Whatever your beliefs, feelings, opinions about those who turn to the street to escape and encounter themselves, know this for certain: reading this narrative is way safer than the reality.

Robert E. Lipscomb
St. Louis, 2006

The View from the Penthouse

Ω

I am on top of the world, or so it seems this bright, clear, brisk morning in the city. I am quite literally on top of this building, due to the fortuitous aspect of my apartment being the penthouse unit with a rooftop access. Terrace, hot tub, potted flowers and all. Perfectly lovely.

The wonderful sound of the passing Metrolink train below, a certain urban song if ever there was one. Not far away, one of the finest hospitals in the nation, evidenced by the constant blaring of ambulance sirens day and night. The music of the city.

Within my line of sight from this eagle's nest is the magnificent façade of our Art Museum, standing majestic and proud in its leafy mantle of Forest Park, an ongoing testament to the culture of this fair community. Also, I can see the curvilinear and columned entrance to the Muny Opera stages, as if arms are reaching out to welcome both thespian and theater-goer. It is magical. I am a prince of the city.

Save for one, tiny miscue in this scene of power and prosperity. I have also in my line of sight my current bank statements and discover to a certain, sickening, sinking dismay that the end is nigh. Downstairs, in a steel fire-file cabinet, reside a couple of thousand dollars, being the last of my ready cash. The remaining few grand in my bank account to be soon consumed by this grand apartment, the Cadillac and my pursuit of the aesthetic lifestyle. It's been one helluva ride.

I know that today I will dress well, as always, drive my great American auto to *The Edge* restaurant, there to be greeted by the buxom, beaming bartender, a sheer beauty in her own right. To sup upon a perfectly prepared Sicilian filet entrée, to sip one or, more likely, three Crown Royals.

I resolve to maintain my posture, as a prince of the city must. I will try my level dog-soldier best to make the brave face, to not become morose and stoop-shouldered, certain of pending doom. Later, I'll cruise the Cadi' one last time to Harrah's, to be distracted by the lights, the sounds, the festive aura.

Maybe, just maybe, I'll win a big jackpot and stave off destruction for a few more weeks. If I could just stave off that greasy-gray Thing encroaching in my mental peripheral vision, the looming confinements of reality.

I am a free man, of the usual sort tolerated by society. A freedom not of joy but of grinding fear, exercising passivity so as not to invoke attention or heated response. It seems better to embrace inertia now, it is best to do nothing. And why not?

Forget about going back to anything called work, paying any attention to whatever investments or business remains. I cannot dissipate the absurdity of it. I fear I am guilty of that greatest social transgression. I have overstayed my welcome at the party of prosperity. The prince of the city is about to be defrocked, his crown of thorns crafted. My head seems to bow as if in readiness to receive it. I don't mean to be flippant, sir, but you're losing your effin' mind. I shall proceed as if everything is going to be alright. The philosophy of plenty, that's for me. But, it isn't going to be alright. Not by a damn shot is anything ever going to be alright, ever again.

I finish lunch, tip too much, (must be a sport about it), and climb back into the welcoming comfort of this great, fine American automobile. Ah, my Cadillac. I have always enjoyed, cherished even, riding behind the crest, as it's said. So, why do I feel so small, right now? Oh, reality sneaking in. A virulent, scabrous pox on all realities! I have no use for such a creation. I find it vexing, obstructive to my overall, headlong pursuit of escape via the aesthetic life.

It was not always so. Once upon a time, in an era of my life from which I have steadfastly main- tained a determined escape velocity, I worshipped other gods. Raised in the 1950's, the middle-son of a middle-salaried man in the middle of a county in the middle of the country. The middle then being judged the balanced point, I suppose. I was the first baby baptized in the new Presbyterian Church in Glendale, Missouri, a church my parents helped found along with three score other families. A Boy Scout tried and true. A playground defender of the smaller, weaker children. Oh, how I relished my role as defeater of the bullies, hero of the trembling cowards who should have learned to respect themselves enough to learn the manly arts of self defense. This comes a s revelation to me now as I perform a similar role as defender of the weak, (being the homeless and nutty), and feel that simmering anger at them simultaneously for not "doing better" in defending their better interests. Oh, well. It seems that I have not ever, really changed over all these decades. I've simply changed the stage.

But, then, I have a somewhat unfair advantage. My father was a Golden Gloves contender, back in the day when that meant something. Usually it meant tough, country kids trying to fight their way out of their world and getting some therapy in the counsels of the ring. I learned at my father's knee or, rather, at his incredible forearms and lightening hands. He never hurt me but I definitely learned to avoid being stung, as they say. My older brother John, whom I worshipped as the perfection of all things male, (he being the beautiful, smart, popular, athletic one), didn't cotton to fisticuffs and my younger brother George came along too late in my father's life for the latter to muster the energy or care to teach the dark arts of pummeling one's adversaries deep into the pavement. I was singular in that regard among my brothers and acquaintances. I would say "peers" but I never did actually meet anyone then who could obtain to that status when it came time to stand-and-deliver-the-good-news.

Enough of this childhood musing, of things past and rightly so. Suffice it to say here that I knew the meaning of personal honor and of giving God his due. Of not always having everything I wanted but always everything I needed. There was love from a good mother and direction from a strong father. I am not a child of blundering or botched parenting. I am reasonably well-educated and an avid reader. No, I have none of the regular, acceptable excuses for what is happening now. As the fiancé of my friend Jay asked me, *"Bob, you seem like a smart guy. What the eff's wrong with you?!?"*

Ah, my dear, 'tis a classic, modern American tale of gaining the world and losing one's soul.

I have somehow, along the way, found myself a child not of Jesus but of Lord Mammon, the latter being a much prettier creature bearing numerous attractions. I suppose I should have seen it coming, but who thinks of such things in this day and age? I'll guess I'll have plenty of time to think about it now, even as time itself is running out.

Damn and double-damn that annoying, dry whisper in the corner of my mind. This whole life, the struggles, victories, defeats, successes, failures, the times of insufficiency, the times of splendid prosperity, none of it means squat. The crackling voice whispers truth, reveals reality, neither of which I desire. *Look here*, it hisses, *all is meaningless as the passing breeze on your face. That's not the cool, refreshing breeze of a bright, promising new day. It's the first breath of cold rage, lurking Death come around to call you in.* Like I should care or be afraid. According to Sir Arthur Conan Doyle, who wrote in his popular novel of the time *The White Company*, I am descended from the young knight's squire who heroically defended the future king of England, Albert, from an attack by wolves, employing only his personal dagger. Ever since, the Lipscomb crest has carried the image of the wolf's head and the dagger in memoriam of this gallant, historic deed. Now another wolf lurks at my door.

Well, then. I am up seventeen stories above Union Boulevard, the same grand way that thousands once crowded to welcome Charles Lindbergh upon his successful return. I could just fly off this rooftop and smash unceremoniously to mushy bits and pieces down below, but what an inconsiderate mess that would be. The Boy Scout in me won't let me leave a place worse than I found it. Besides, I just spent a small fortune on crowns for several teeth and I won't waste all that money and pain for a 200 foot blacktop stop. So, jumping is out. Evil gods demand that I remain alive and present. Strip away all material possessions and opportunities for distraction. Now they have my undivided attention, but I'd rather not hear what they have to say, thank you.

Well, at least I still have one old, if not dear, acquaintance left. It plays back to one other small, troubling factoid regarding my previously mentioned childhood. There has always been this greasy-gray shroud just around the edges of my mental peripheral vision. This sort-of soul shroud, spiritually threatening, repressive THING, always and never quite there. All attempts to elude, evade, outrun, escape and evict it from my mind, from my spirit, have failed miserably. Alas, 'ole chum, I see you stayed with me through every twist and turn, foray and jaunt. You may be the only thing I truly know, familiar if not welcome. The Devil I know rather than the fresh demons waiting just outside my soon-to-be vacated penthouse door. The great demon of failure, of surrender. I wish most, not for the return of prosperity, although that would be comforting, of course. No, I wish most that I eff'n cared.

I fall back slowly like one of those slow-motion movie scenes into this greasy-gray Thing. It takes me into its sinewy, greasy, unholy embrace.

Folks who fancy themselves professionals in such matters of the mind will later call it depression, despair, existential ennui. (If they're so smart, how come the world is more screwed up than ever?)

This Thing, lacking any enchantments, offering no promise save that of misery, this crown piece on the efforts of a lifetime. Ennui, my ass. I close my eyes and drift into its embrace like encountering that lover you know is all wrong for you but nonetheless irresistible.

The ambulance sirens carve their path, the Metrolink train clacks by, birds chirp, breeze blows. Nothing. Absolutely nothing is the same as it was nor will it be again. The wolf is loose.

*

9/11: The Inevitable War

Ω

I am sitting in what has come to be known to my memory as the interim apartment. That place of prosperity's purgatory that isn't Heaven nor quite Hell. A two-room affair in a decent neighborhood, my having returned to the community of my youth like a creature returns to its spawning place. It's familiar if not comfortable. I have given up on resolutions of possibility, the sloppy artistry of my life revealed full force. The very concept of hope has escaped unscathed from my reality, from my consciousness. I reside within my conscious madness, imagining there is some manner of existence that lies just beyond freedom.

I turn on the TV, (my final, remaining mode of distraction). The news is on, but it seems too late in the morning for that. Ah, some Special Report. Probably another bus bombing in Israel, some school children shot up by one of their classmates or, that ultimate banality, another local priest caught dallying with his choirboys.

17

No, wait, this is something else. Good, it may be entertaining. Lots of smoke and running about, yes, I recognize the scene now, that's New York City. Now I see the report that four airliners have gone missing, a certain euphemism employed by the sentinels of the public's emotional stability, when what they really mean is hundreds of people have died in airplane crashes. I reason that this is no accident, too many airplanes at the same time. This is enemy action. (You know the Rule: *Once is an accident, twice is a coincidence, three times is enemy action. Four times and you're getting your ass kicked.*)

The President, aka, the Commander in Chief, is busy flying about in parts unknown exercising his right to survive and fight another day. The fact of this telling me that we are at war. Real war. Not that death-by-a-thousand-cuts kind of thing that's been going on for decades now. No, the real deal, where huge and prepared adversaries who hate your living guts are set about killing you, burning down your cities and murdering your children at every opportunity. I am shocked but not surprised. How so?

This is the war I always knew would come. This is the moment in history when everything I have been distracting myself with for years, you know, prosperity and party, has been ultimately revealed as futile and foolhardy. The whole world knows it now, not just me. All this stuff we do to build ourselves up, to imagine ourselves kings of the Earth, it's mostly bullshit. It's mostly just a bunch of junk that will quickly rust and rot away, but not before our hearts have rusted over from lack of use, not before our minds/spirits have rotted away. It's easy for me to see the motivations of our adversaries. They hate us for our excesses, disdain us for not paying attention. Well, you've got our attention now. May God help you 'cause the Devil will have his due.

I am not surprised because this is the Great War, the changer of societies, that I always believed/knew would come. As a child, I practiced ducking under wood school desks and in stairwells to survive the imminent nuclear blast launched by the Soviets or the Red Chinese. Presidents and potential Presidents gunned down. Leaders of the

19

people and champions of freedom gunned down. A long and dirty war fought for who knows what ending in exhaustion of both bodies and spirits. This is the war I always knew would come. But, how did it know to begin concurrent with my own personal malaise? Maybe I somehow always believed deep inside that everything was so fragile, contingent, absurd and therefore made the choices I did, lived the life I have. Knowing that it would all end anyway.

I watch the great building suddenly begin to collapse, pancaking down one story upon another. People on fire choosing to leap to their death rather than roast slowly upon this hellfire of man's making. The greasy-gray shroud envelopes the surrounding buildings and fleeing people. Ah, I have seen you before. My mind's shroud has come around to live large and conquer the world.

*

Grasping at His Hemline

Ω

9/11 is a few days past now. The hubbub is slowly passing even while the nation's leaders declare eternal war. I decide to walk the mile or so to the church of my origins, the one founded with the help of my now-long deceased father. It's a chilly day and my legs have not really been so exercised in a long time. I was in manifestations past a sergeant of combat infantry, so I know on a decent level what a good feeling walking evokes. I stride along the sidewalk, it's a clear day, save in my mind of course. Fear stalks along my path as I try to decide whether I really want to meet the pastor of Glendale Presbyterian Church today, or not. How does one enter the building holding a lifetime of memories, reflections and ancient acquaintances and declare personal failure, spiritual devastation and existential despair? Not exactly a hero's homecoming here.

Nevertheless, I climb the steps to the white doors of the sanctuary building and enter as I have done thousands of times before. Inquiring of the secretary in the little operations office if I could just have a few moments of the Pastor's time, it would be very much appreciated thank you. She picks of the phone and announces my presence. I am almost immediately greeted by the Pastor and ushered into her office.

Pastor Nancy Rowland, a sturdy woman, fiftyish, beaming a great smile that reads genuine all the way to me. The conversation ensues.

Pastor Nancy: *Good morning! How can I be of service to you today? What's troubling you?*

(Ah, since I haven't seen you since your mother's funeral, what the heck are you looking for now?)

Me: *My life appears to be falling apart in short order and it just seemed a good and safe place to come to, to find some friends for a brief moment, some sanctuary, as it were.*

Pastor Nancy: *That's good of you, you know instinctively where to turn in times of trouble. Is there some specific thing you'd like to talk about today?*

Me: *Well, I have screwed up just about everything I've touched recently and it appears, no it's definite, that I'll be essentially homeless in the next week or so and out on the street.*

Pastor Nancy: (She looks shocked. The son of one of the founding members of this church, a decorated military veteran, a Glendale kid…out on the street? Huh?) *That's terrible! How did this come to be?* (Not really looking for that extra-lengthy explanation, I surmise.) *How can I help you?*

Me: *I'm not sure. I just wanted to be someplace friendly, familiar, safe.*

Pastor Nancy sits quietly, appraising, her lips moving slightly as if attempting to form some adequate answer for all this. *You're always welcome here.* She smiles. It is nearing the end of this encounter. *Please seek me out whenever you need support or spiritual guidance and anything for that matter.*

I take her quite literally at her word and then I blurt the most remarkable, in a potentially-nutty kind of way, observation.

Me: *I am most worried about the bluejays and cardinals who have come to rely on me to put out crumbled up old bread when it's snowing or really cold.*

I almost come to tears, I feel them welling up. Oh, Jeez, don't make anymore of a fool of yourself than you already have.

Pastor Nancy: *That's good! You see, that even in the midst of your own terrible problems and needs, you are greatly concerned with the needs of others, of the innocent, of God's beautiful creations!*

Good save! She pulled out one great priestly pronouncement and saved my crumbling self-esteem with her answer. Affirmation. Good stuff! I feel re-emboldened just a little bit, no doubt I sit up a little straighter in her very comfortable padded guest chair with the those strong arms upon which both of my elbows are depending and firmly planted.

The conversation should end now, on this high note, and it does. I rise and she doesn't hesitate to follow. But hen she startles me by advancing into my space and hugging me with a great hug. I can't remember my last hug. Certainly not a sincere one.

Most definitely not by a priest, Presbyterian or otherwise. I am surprised, a bit embarrassed. Oddly warmed.

It was good thing to come here. I promise (or threaten) to come back if I should need to. Pastor Nancy smiles sympathetically and re-affirms my welcome there anytime. Two affirmations in one morning. Maybe things are starting to turn around.

I take my leave and stride back to my little apartment, my way-station between Heaven and Hell. I'm heading into society's version of Hell, called poverty and invisibility. The living ghost existence. But, I am encouraged. I feel stronger than I have felt in a very long time. As I have virtually nothing, how can this be? Choosing not to examine this too closely right now, I begin selecting which items can fit in my backpack, which will contain the sum total of my earthly possessions for the future to come. It's okay. I've lugged backpacks before with nothing but a few articles of clothing and a melting Snickers bar. No M16 rifle to comfort me this time.

The worst part of it all is that this time, on this grand adventure, there will be no mighty Army to service and support my expedition. Nobody will be sending reinforcements. Later, over many months, Pastor Nancy will drive through all kinds of weather in a beat-up, old car all the way downtown to meet me at Union Station, for lunch, for conversation, for some kind of human contact with a reasonably sane person, (her, not me.) She even forks over some cash from time to time and it makes a huge difference in both the quality of my life physically but, most telling, in the quality, re-birth really, of my spirit. Pastor Nancy proves to be the "real deal" among priests. Some part of my life is owed to her. Forever.

No reinforcements are coming...Except, maybe Pastor Nancy and an army called The Church.

*

God Loves a Good Pair of Shoes

Ω

One of the very first, most important things, the aspiring hobo should do is apprize his collection of footgear and select only the two most useful pairs to accompany him on the coming great adventure. This is more easily said than accomplished if one happens to have been previously prosperous and therein acquired a number of fine shodding for one's feet. As I may have remarked before, I possess a vast body of experience regarding the proper selection of footgear for any proposed mission. As a former sergeant of infantry, I know that what one wears on one's feet can mean the difference between victory and defeat. (No pun, here.) God Himself loves a good pair of shoes.

To transform a common little suffering of the long march into a glorious, even exemplary, suffering, select a quality set of shoes. In my case, that came down to two pairs; the first being Rockports and the second being Reebock athletic shoes. The Rockports had this metal spine down the middle that

27

really made for some sure-footed going and the Reebocks were just the ticket for summer strolls up and down the sidewalks of St. Louis. Up and down, up and down, up and down, you get the picture.

Those Rockports lasted nearly two years. Jay Swoboda snapped a photograph of them and we wrote a letter of commendation to the Rockport people heralding their quality product. They didn't answer. I guess the image of hoboes everywhere preferring their product isn't the branding strategy they have in mind. *Scene from Rockport commercial:* Bearded, scraggly, stinky bum with flies around his head and his pants tied on with a length of frayed rope sticks his foot in camera's lens for close-up of the beaten-up pair of Rockports he so cherishes. *Dialogue:*

I can walk from my drug rehab to grab a free bologna san'wich and then hike up to the quickstore to hoist a tall-boy before I have to run away from the bicycle cops for peein' on a park tree in plain sight of two nuns at High Mass! (Hey! Don't blame for peein' in public...Didn't I tell ya about the tall-boy beer I just drunk? Pay attention here!) AND, not only that, our exuberant proponent of proper footgear exhorts, *Urine doesn't even stain the fine leather of these here shoes!* Not exactly, what the Rockport folks are looking for, I guess. Kind of goes against that whole wiry-strong mountain biker in the Northwest skidding to a halt before his lithe, young girlfriend. All freshness and good health. Wait! That's it! I have it now: *Wear Rockports as you hike hundreds of miles throughout the city, all as part of The Hobo Health-plan. Get fit! Get Rockports!*

Maybe not.

Thanks anyway. These shoes are great and, being a most-of-the-time Christian, I know God loves a good pair of shoes.

*

The Valkyries Fly to My Rescue

Ω

Thus properly shod, backpack stuffed, heart for the journey emboldened by the counsel of a true priest, I set out one fine, bright January day for whatever lay ahead. It is precisely January 13th. As a former sometime gambler, that should be off-putting to me. But, I am remarkably unafraid, more curious than anything. Life's all about the experiencing, isn't it? Having bought every kind of experience known to modern man, what manner of adventure may be acquired when one has nothing to spend at all?

I do what comes naturally to me. I head for a church, in this case, one that is seven miles away and reconstituted as an outpost of that venerable organization known as The Salvation Army. All parts of that name sound good to me. Salvation. Army. Yep, I can relate to both of those concepts.

Somewhere around mile two-and-a-half my body informs me that I may be trying to write a check my level of fitness can't cash. I am, after all, 51, not 31. I remain a powerful sergeant of infantry, Army of the United States, only in my head, which, as we have discovered, may not be functioning at optimal levels lately. By the grace of God and the amusement of the Devil, I reach my destination late in the afternoon. It is my first few hours without the accustomed security of a home to go to, a toilet at my convenience, a kitchen full of good and not-so-good for me stuff. (How I used to relish cruising through Schnuck's, buying anything I saw that looked amusing, often giving away items later to the, *oh s--t,* Salvation Army!)

The young woman working the desk in her tiny office welcomes me with a look of genuine puzzlement. That's the second time that's happened. It won't be the last by a long shot. Being derived of ancient Celtic blood via the Norman-Saxon English and Scots, I surmise I can verily read her thoughts. What does this well-groomed, clean, dressed by Famous Barr, middle-aged man want here? I rush to remedy her confusion. I am just now out on the street, and was wondering what guidance or services you might provide. She ever-so-slightly smiles. She thinks I'm kidding her, like I'm the Salvation Army's version of a secret-shopper testing her skills. Yes, madam, I want to say, this is a quality control exercise, so you better look sharp! She pulls out a couple of brief forms, instructs me in their completion, blinks at least twice at what I have filled in. Your 51 years old? You're college-educated? You're a decorated veteran? You are dead broke? Yep. Ain't it grand! Now, what you got for me, woman? She coolly reaches for the telephone and instantly I am struck with the idea she is calling the police to remove this vagabond impersonator from her midst. But, no, she relays my presence and current situation to someone on the other end of the line. Glancing up she announces that someone from the "outreach" services, (whatever that is), is coming to pick me up. Um, okay. Where are we going? She'll take you to one of the men's shelters for the evening until you can sort things out later.

This comes as a revelation to me. First, that there are shelters for guys experiencing what I am and secondly that someone will actually come and fetch me and chauffeur me to a safe place. Who knew? Certainly not this old prince of the city, this who- even- wants- to know- about- this- crap kind of guy.

An hour passes. The sun has disappeared to be replaced by a cold breeze and overcast sky. As if the weather can judge my moods and respond accordingly. It reminds me of when I was a little boy laying in the grass looking up at puffy white clouds imagining that I could move the clouds and make them form various shapes simply by my mind power, my will that it be so.

My chauffeur arrives. It is a middle-aged woman who, while not exactly smiling, presents a non-threatening countenance. She is accompanied by a strongish-looking black man, I figure him for the heavy of the group. Mess with this woman and I f—k you up. With a general understanding of our roles in this world securely obtained, I climb into her SUV and off we go. My Valkyrie has flown to my rescue, to carry me to the Valhalla of the Warrior Dead. Well, anyway, a nice lady has arrived to transport the societal deceased to their next abode. Close enough.

It turns out to be an eye-opening ride. One of the worst of my life and that's saying something. You think boarding a hot, suffocating bus for the long ride to Army bootcamp is unnerving? You think losing all your worldly possession, (or, in my case, just giving the s—t away), is unsettling? Whew, then just wait until you ride to your first encounter with a shelter for homeless men. Jesus. Ungood.

My Valkyrie's name is Joann. She patiently drives all over the City in parts I would not have previously ventured into even with my aforementioned M16. From feeling saved and somewhat euphoric over the prospects of arriving reinforcements, I am crushed in my chest, my head is being squeezed by some hideous, invisible pressure. It is the end of me. Not just spiritually, but now most certainly physically as well. I am not up for this. I am not the brave soldier of my youth. I am older than I've ever been. Thousands of years old, crumbling to dust like some forlorn Egyptian mummy, alive only by some terrifically evil incantation. I have always prides myself on maintaining my personal responsibility to everything I could to uphold the idea of what it means to be a true man. I am on the precipice of achieving complete failure in this matter.

We cruise by three of the men's shelters in the city. The first is operated by her husband, one Tom Burnham, the second is the Salvation Army facility which looks to me to be duly guarded by human Ceres and the third shelter appearing so nondescript as to be possible not real, a movie lot façade, a Hansel and Gretel ploy to lure in unsuspecting individuals to some grisly doom.

I implore Joann to return me to Kirkwood. I have some cash left. I'll just buy some small foodstuffs and re-think this whole thing.

I've always been good like that. Using my mental acuity to escape various situations minimally scathed.

She complies, remarkably driving me all the way back out of the city. She turns to me as I drag-

flow out of her SUV and quietly informs me: *"It's a hard thing."*

Her words drive like a nail into my mind. Simple. Complete. Wisdom born of vast experience. I know it to be true but I am just. not. ready. yet.

I will later walk up to the local Steak-n-Shake and there drink cup after cup of coffee throughout that night.

For the first time I can recall, I am afraid. Truly afraid.

*

I Succumb to Shelter

Ω

I am fresh out of tricks now. I've used every all night diner I can find. I've hung out in libraries all day long. I have not slept a total of six good hours in three, (or is it five?) days. I return to the original Salvation Army church after a grueling hike of many, many miles. I comprehend that I am physically weakened by deprivation of both sleep and proper nourishment. My will to resist the life I so consciously chose through surrender after surrender has waned. I have gone from that not-caring which is merely mental to that not-caring that comes upon the defeated.

Dutifully, like a patient angel, without expressing "I told you so" or any other judgment, Jo-ann arrives to once again take me to a shelter. She uses her cellphone to go around usual protocols about placing new arrivals in shelters and calls her husband directly. He instructs me in the procedures, Jo Anne drives by the large, black door in the basement of a huge, Gothic edifice on the south part of

37

the City. Some place called Peter and Paul. I wonder silently if one must be Catholic to be accepted here.

It grinds into my soul that I am truly poor now. A state of life not ever imagined or anticipated. I always thought I could escape this sort of thing. I am, or was, a middle-class kid with a decent education, a loyal son, loves his God, the Good Soldier. How could this happen? It's real now. It's repressive reality upon me completely. I'm just another nigger, I guess, One of those sad sack bearded bums I used to laugh at and momentarily consider bumping into with the Cadi' when they'd defiantly cross my path while jaywalking in the middle of the street.

At least it's an experience. A new one. One I haven't completely consciously crafted to allow for exits at my will and command. Any lights I perceive on this particular ring of Hell reveal themselves to be merely additional entrances back into the ring. How can this be? How can this still be the America I struggled to defend? What strange, loathsome land have I unwittingly discovered?

This is not just wandering, tune in, turn on, drop out. Some insidious surgery has been performed on my soul and I have died accordingly. This feast of lesser saints involving demons and the carrion my body, my life's history.

Thus ends my illusion of fair play, of justice, of order. I always knew that material possessions were mostly crap but this tossing away of human beings, this shutting away of the ghostmen, this is too appalling, too wrong. This is turning out to be the peregrinatio of purposelessness.

Beamed not up but down, I am the new possession of an alien power.

I enter the shelter. One must descend a steep flight of steps to the shelter floor. Of course. Hell is always downward, isn't it? It is beyond noisy, voices raised in banter, complaints, hailing one another. Bedlam. This is not helped by the concrete basement walls shiny with some cretinous form of mold.

I sign in, choose a bunk. The men here are overwhelmingly black, under the influence of something or other and not loving us white guys, especially old white guys like yours truly. I shouldn't be concerned with this. Didn't I play football with my black brothers? Didn't I hunker down in foxholes on combat teams? Didn't I mourn Martin Luther King with them? But, that was so long ago and the world has changed. These aren't my old teammates or combat buddies. These are the New Breed, the thundercats of the age. Climb in fully clothed and pull the blanket over me. It is not late in the evening. The TV blares. The voices rise and fall. It's not as bad as some Army barracks I've been in, but it's crummy enough.

Then surprising me and I am twice surprised as I did not believe I had surprise left in me, I am calm. Peaceful. I suppose much like the dead who have finally accepted the reality of their non-life status. I go to sleep. With any luck, I won't wake up.

*

Whats Up Jay

Ω

Weeks pass at Peter and Paul men's shelter. The routine of arising at 5 AM and hitting the streets by 6 AM is becoming acceptable. The only bad days are when it's raining or the temperature has dropped and the wind has come up. It being the winter of 2002, things have been reasonably mild. I count that as a lucky thing as I grasp at any indicators of potential change of fortune.

Occasionally, some goodhearted group arrives at dinner time bringing some yummy, home baked dishes. Never did I see a bunch of rowdy, usually rude guys quiet down like they do when some nice church ladies come trooping in with hot dishes emitting delectable aromas. Once in a rare while, some preachers-in-training would show up to regale us poor sinners with the Good News. It is invariably in the old Roman style, you know, accusatory, blame-setting, insulting. Don't they realize Jesus came for such as us? The poor, the downtrodden, oh we of little faith? But God in his infinite mercy stretches forth his right hand, or possibly the back of his left hand, and eventually swats the itinerant preachers away. Perhaps God allows in his mighty wisdom the insufferable little men to come and spout among us in order that we might more fully recognize and appreciate the silence that comes as a blessed, freshening breeze in the immediate moments following the exit of those miserable, little men. As if, we aren't trapped well enough already. Surely, it's a violation of the Geneva Accords to be regaled by these fools. Amen.

So, it is with a collective and audible sigh of relief when we see arriving one evening, rather than the aforementioned Boors for Christ, a bevy of lovely, clearly collegiate men and women, all bright and spiffy shined.

It is a fellow named Jay Swoboda, accompanied by some Washington University students on a mission, of some kind. And, so begins a new day in the life of this wandering soul, yours truly. Jay has a proposal and it is this: *You guys on the street will write your stories. I will print them in this new street magazine. You will then also sell said magazine and keep the money received for yourself!* This strikes me as eminently reasonable and, more importantly, actually doable. Only a small group sign up to sell the magazine but the game is afoot, nonetheless.

Having always used writing as therapy, as well as the briefly mentioned gambit of getting girls to like me, I sign on with great enthusiasm. Here is the first light I've seen that is not just another entry into Hell. This could be the way out of the situation I so eagerly, if subconsciously, created. I can tell the stories, help myself, help others, proclaim the real good news of God's work in this world here and now, all distractions from His teaching me whatever needs to be learned long removed, that I am alive at least in some form, battered for sure, not quite dead but whose opinion is that...Yes, I can do this. It is the first moment in my sojourn upon the cold streets of a struggling city that I can actually say that and believe it.

I can do this.

*

A Life in the Night

Ω

This article originally appeared in Whats Up magazine. It is the first piece written by Robert E. Lipscomb and won the NASNA 2003 Award for nonfiction writing.

Having become accustomed to referring to denizens of the demimonde as bums, crazies and the like, I find myself now haunting the same habitat – sometimes dazed, often amazed, at the length, breadth and depth of variety among the homeless personalities encountered.

Some are truly bums in the most derogatory sense of the term, but most are not. Some are definitely "nuts," but again, while some element of mental or spiritual malaise is present, most street people are not looming predators who scope for their big chance to pounce on some hapless passerby. In fact, avoidance behavior is more often demonstrated than annoying incursions into one's personal space, as evidenced, say, in aggressive panhandling or simply passing by the unwashed vagabond.

No longer able to remotely rebuke *"them"*, I find, to my frustration and humiliation, that *"they"* must now be addressed as *"we"* and not *"them"*, (alone and comfortably distant), but *me,* now ever present among them in similar straits.

I once was quite prosperous, if not exactly rich. Now, I'm dead broke. How may I engage in knowledgeable debate with others of similar ilk over, for instance, the true provenance of a boloney sandwich: *Is it from New Life Evangelistic or Peter & Paul?* The latter service being evidently vastly superior in freshness and often accompanied by cheese, as all self-respecting baloney sandwiches should be. Such discussions occasionally devolve into tangential tirades such as *"Why baloney? Why not real food?!?"* Especially, when it is suspected, by those in the know about such arcane matters, that the person who provided such insalubrious sustenance probably drove over to the homeless shelter in a Lexus SUV, and that said person still glistened with sweat obtained from a healthy workout in a posh gym whose annual membership fees are sufficient to feed a hungry herd of hoboes for a fortnight.

Hoboes. We, (yes, I said *we*, not *they*), often refer to each other with this sobriquet, both as bond and rebuke, no doubt much to the chagrin of the aforementioned Lexus liberal who would find such terminology offending all rules of politically-correct decorum. Screw 'em. Political correctness is just one more luxury we can't afford, best left to the nasty-neat's eye-rolling expressions of faux disgust. There, I feel much better now. So ends the obligatory outburst of class conflict.

Truly, the street folks I've come to know are among the most appreciative, thankful, faith-filled folks anywhere. Here, small things really matter. In this is a certain, quiet wisdom. Heart.

In a daily exercise of street-smart bricolage, the "average", (there is no such creature), concrete-commando gathers whatever he may from wide and often ingenious sources. The hunt for such arcane items as a fresh pair of socks, bus ticket, a cigarette and, the most holy of Grails, a bed in a decent shelter, proves a certain cunning wit to be the rule rather than the exception. Evidenced constantly is a native grace concerning the necessity of meeting and beating truth in its wilder states. The bum-bricoleur as profound rather than pathetic. In this on-going tragicomedy, the newly minted homeless person is actually looked down upon by the experienced or, if you prefer, professionally homeless, as incompetent dilettantes. Encompassing all, however, is the quiet understanding that no control of any real power exists in the unfolding of each new day. It will be what it will be. This is the day the Lord hath made, rejoice and be glad in it or go eff yourself.

One deals with whatever and moves on. No glory, little reward, no guarantees. Real as real can be. Surreal may be a better description. The kind of nauseating realization that tends to sicken and terrify any thinking person, especially when the day dawns but brings no warmth, just continuing freezing wind, or soaking rain, or spirit-sapping heat and empty plans.

A refrain from an old Seal tune bangs through my brain over and over like some bad-ass psychological MP3 download. *"We're never gonna survive, unless we get a little bit crazy..."* Normal life, to draw upon a continuing musical metaphor, is Side A of life's record. The B Side is something that should never have been created in God's studio and never played on these streets. Homelessness is the B Side of the record of life.

Well, it's almost lunchtime. Time to leave my adopted offices at table three of the Fine Arts department in the Central Library and stroll over to St. Patrick's for yet another free meal. (If you're starving to death in St. Louis, you're a moron. Truly.) There is a small but dedicated band of true people of faith who consistently and unwaveringly provide meals for those in need of nourishment, both for the body and the spirit. Go. Seek. Find.

Along the way there is a commotion on the sidewalk just ahead. An absolutely artless and robustly bad street character has managed to attract special attention to his cause. Bevies of bicycle cops flutter around him like blue flies on a shit pile. The kind of ne'er- do- well that inspire city fathers to dream of closing local shelters and herding the homeless to the remote industrial outback. For every such hobo, one hundred decent hoboes struggle unobtrusively to just survive another day. This, in a nation of wealth and power. I can scarcely abide it. These are our fellow citizens, Americans all, screwed down by economic or cultural forces, and forces of Hell itself inside their minds, sometimes weird, often artless, intelligently primal. Fractal souls. Robustly delicate. Humanly precious. Real.

*

Club Cathedral

Ω

Hoboes have this tendency, due to the fear of scarcity, to withhold information among each other as to the location of any newly rumored resource. It is only by listening to this *sotto voce* communication that I learn of an intriguing, new source of morning sustenance and refuge from the weather. You see, even if you have the luxury of a bed in the local shelter, you will still be thrown out into the pre-dawn dark every morning. Stared at by roving police patrols, lacerated by the quiet laughter of passing motorists. So it is that finding a morning refuge becomes a primary mission, a key element to surviving intact on the streets.

I overhear that some place called Christ Church Cathedral has donuts for the taking and cups of hot coffee. Free, no less. But, and here's the rub, it's very limited and those who know will be on it like, well, flies on shit. I decide to buzz by looking to score some pastry and hot java.

Where the heck is this Cathedral place? That big building out on Lindell? No, it's that church in the middle of the city. Oh, that one, the one that always made me wonder why anyone would choose to build such an edifice in the middle of a crumbling city. Later, I discover it's been here for something like 150 years and the city grew up around it. Still, why stay here, amidst boarded-up buildings and pigeon-crap caked sidewalks? Go figure.

I enter through some doors off an essentially vacant parking lot to din a small hallway already full of hungryhungryhoboes (that jingle regarding some cereal commercial with hippos adapting nicely.) The smell of unwashed humanoids and hot donuts assaults my nostrils accompanied by the ever-present din of twenty idiots talking at once. Some woman strides purposefully from down the corridor and orders the assembled heathens to quiet down, this is a place of business, a church. Respect it! They quiet down. She turns away satisfied to disappear into some warren.

A wiry, black guy emerges from a galley kitchen with a tray of warm donuts. Instantly and without invitation or etiquette apparent, the hungry horde descends like maddened locusts onto the donut tray. Fully a third of said pastries fall in bits and pieces to the floor as filthy hands greedily grub for their presumed fair share. Somehow, I've suddenly lost my appetite. This is too much. At least, now I know where the expression "bum rush" comes from. One obese, short, semi-Hispanic female immediately threatens to cut somebody if they don't back off. Too late. The morning's offerings are long gone. Even the coffee is getting spilled, mostly by quaking hands belonging to the extraordinarily intoxicated and/or crack-smoking, red-eyed demons present. Fairly speaking, really, they don't qualify as demons. They couldn't make the cut. Every echelon has their own performance criteria, their bar that must be hurdled to quality as one of the gang. Nope. This bunch doesn't even qualify as demon apprentices. There are real servants of Satan out here, but not here this morning. I have absolutely no doubt, based on what I have seen in the past dark months, that that Great Demon will appear someday, probably right here in this church. He's disrespectful like that, you know. I'm guessing He won't listen to the imprecations of the nice church lady to quiet down.

The donuts are gone, the coffee expended. However, the secret's out now and I will surely return here tomorrow to try again. If nothing else, it's been entertaining. Still, I can't help but continue to wonder just what the heck is this church doing in this place, in this time? What are they all about? It's a vexing curiosity. They have annoyed me on some level by their presence.

In my mind, some candle has been lit and I'm just the foolish moth they're looking for. I'll be back. You haven't seen the last of me yet. Poor bastards.

*

Rising Up

Ω

To wander the streets of St. Louis is at once an entertaining prospect, even for the completely poor. My spirit is lifted up along with my eyes when I spy out some new architectural pediment that I didn't see before when just driving through. My present circumstances at least afford me the purchase of well-crafted public art that many of these old buildings present. As a suburban kid, I had believed the city to be a place of grayness, dirt and danger and surely there is plenty of that. But, there is, I now can see, so much more here. It sort of fills me up with new oxygen; the swift breezes caused by the dam effect of the buildings clears away some of the persistent cobwebs of my mind. Oh, now I see. Yes, now I hear. Not perfectly yet, but soon. Or maybe just the promise of soon.

I am fortunate in many ways, even while standing here dead broke. It is time to linger and watch a while. Seated upon the cold, concrete bench-like extensions on the outside of the Central Library building, (just across the street from that mysterious church), I see workmen ripping the boards off some of the great, old buildings. I hear hammers ringing out and ripsaws carving out new things, new opportunities, perhaps. Everywhere, in the midst of all this human despair wandering around here, rings the sound of hope or maybe just the potential for hope. Someone somewhere has decided to plunge a huge bunch of money into fixing up this old town for some new use. It is so clearly purpose-filled that I cannot help but catch some of its spirit. It's so purposeful, so hopeful, so obviously risky. I am lured by the risk-taking, of course. I come to love the ring of hammers, the drills, the saws, the thumping street paving machines ripping out the old boulevards to make way for the new. Something big is happening here. Who'd a guessed it? Here. St. Louis. This old dog has come 'round to hunt some more and its quarry is the biggest game of all. *A new, urban destiny.* I drink in its temerity to dare fate. With every hammer's blow I hear, I gather in strength.

Just across the way from the Library is a small, green space embraced by some fine, old trees. Its official name is Lucas Park. It is known on the street as Hobo Park for its nearly constant use by local homeless folks. It sits directly adjacent to a pricey childcare center. To me, it represents everything about the life and history of this city, all abbreviated into this one, little place.

Here, you can still find the outlines of the common fields of old St. Louis, if you know how to look. Just picture the areas bounded by Olive, Locust, St. Charles and Washington avenues as open fields and orchards. Once upon a time, the wealthy citizens of our fair town decided to build upon what once where the common fields a new, residential sanctuary to escape the "undesirable conditions" of the burgeoning City. They called their new residential fortress Lucas Place.

The gateway to this special place was a small park then known as Missouri Park or Sunken Garden park. The area became home to the city's premier cultural and religious institutions. Here could be

found the First Presbyterian Church, with the prestigious private school called Mary Institute, along with
the Episcopal Christ Church Cathedral, (the donut
place...), the Methodist Centenary Church and even
a Jewish house of worship called The Temple of the
Gates of Truth.

By the late 1880's, prestigious Lucas Place had
all but vanished, with only the Hazlett Campbell
House as sole surviving representative of the grand
mansions of the day. The wealthy had once again
moved westward to the new private enclaves of the
Central West End, leaving behind row upon row of
boarding houses that became the living quarters of
the working class that provided the laborers for
mostly garment trades headquartered along Washington Avenue. Missouri Park was re-named Lucas
Park. Workers living nearby would flock on typically
muggy summer evenings and weekends to the cooler
oasis of the small, sunken garden in their midst. For
scores of decades to follow, Lucas Park's primary
function would be to serve the poor and working
folks until, one day, no one really knows exactly

when, it became known, unofficially of course, as Hobo Park.

Flanked by a dilapidating structure that originally housed a YWCA but now serves as a shelter for the homeless and magnet for those seeking various social services, and the elegant headquarters of the Public Library, and the venerable Christ Church Cathedral and row upon row of once vibrant but now vacant, dangerous and foreboding loft buildings, Lucas park became a sanctuary again, not this time for the wealthy but rather for exactly the opposite social class; the destitute, the homeless and the street thugs that pray upon them. Then the re-developers arrived. Now, nothing can be the same as it was. The hammers ring out the Good News as surely as the bells of the Cathedral. A new day is upon us.

This city, once believed dead, old news, useless, is rising up from the grave. I take it as personally speaking to me, as God's way of showing me, the ever obtuse and densest of His children, that there is always hope, if you just lay your hands to it.

The mighty arms of the carpenters are my arms. The courage of the rich men will become part of my courage. A rising tide lifts all boats if we are but brave enough to launch upon it.

For the first time in a long time, I begin to believe again. I am at the right place, at the right time. The city of my birth is rising up and I have resolve to rise up with it. I, too, will try to create something new, something worthwhile. Not a mere repetition of my old life, but something new and of lasting worth. The city and I will rise up together to claim our new, urban destiny. A destiny of both substance and soul.

The pen will be my hammer, words will be my paint. And, maybe, the gates to the temple of truth will slowly rise again. *Selah.*

*

Mitch

Ω

The idea to feed the downtown homeless has taken off, big time. The good folks at this mysterious church in the middle of the city, Christ Church Cathedral, have opted to expand the bagels-and-coffee morning repast into the hallways of their administration building known as the Bishop Tuttle Memorial building. Which is amusing to me because this Bishop Tuttle character looks quite severe and disapproving of hosting a hundred ne'er do-wells in his building. At least that's what the stone effigy on the wall overlooking the hallway says to me.

Anyway, amidst the near-bedlam of this morning gathering are the church workers and volunteers who set it all up and interact with the, um, clients. I am beginning to learn most of their names and who can be talked to and who'd rather not. I call this "talking to grownups" because conversation with the usual assortment of street characters is a waste of the art. Perhaps we are not all mad but just focusing on our own private internal vision. Whatever, it's a good exercise for whatever remaining mental faculties I possess and an opportunity to express myself without the usual street vernacular involving a vulgarity every third word. Hoboes are the ultimate withholders, that being the only remaining power. So, I evade their artifice and mumblings to engage normal people, just to practice in case I should ever reside in their midst on a more regular basis. When in Rome...

Among the nice church ladies I have learned to engage and trust on some level is Sharon. She's whip smart, occasionally bawdy, obviously possessing a certain street-smarts of her own, yet a professional person in healthcare. Right now, as always when it's her turn to serve here, we strike up conversation and just now she's introducing me to a handsome, teenager who is evidently her nephew. A curly-haired boy with an old-soul's face. Let me explain this.

Out on the streets, one must possess an ability to almost instantly discern where the next person is coming from, his attitude, his intentions. It gets into the realm more of feelings than evidence. If you wait for actual evidence, it may be too late. This discernment must be decided upon with the other person no closer than three-quarters of a city block away. Then, if necessary, you can puff up your feathers and look more formidable or make small and avoid contact altogether. Make the wrong call here and pay the price in blood and broken bone. It's not that much different from battlefield situational awareness. You veterans know the old rule: *Be polite, be professional. Be ready, willing and able to kill every motherfucker you meet.* Seems rather harsh to me nowadays.

But I digress. This young guy Mitch is personable and non-threatening, the first thing to be discerned. But, and this is just my own musing on the subject, he's also not really here. This is not unusual among the ghostmen of the street but this is the first time I have experienced it among the normal folks of the world, especially one so young. Hence, the old-soul judgment. He's been here before. Planet Earth, I mean. In some previous, multiple incarnations and some part of him knows, (as opposed to merely believing,) that he is here but for awhile, just sort of passing through. As it happens, that's exactly what he's doing here this morning. His aunt Sharon has brought him with her, both as child-tending duty and certain introduction to the B-side of life.

Somewhere in the middle of the morning, the hallways now filled with a rather dense air and a hundred humans sucking all the oxygen out of the atmosphere, Sharon asks, implores, me to show her nephew Mitchell where St. Patrick's is located. (St. Patrick's is the megacenter of social services in downtown St. Louis.)

I am at once struck with a number of emotional responses. A millisecond may be overstating the elapsed time here. First, what the eff does this woman think I'm doing here? Babysitting services? And, no, it's cold and drizzly outside and I'd rather not go out into it. Again. Layered atop all that is a surprising sense of personal pride. This nice church lady, clearly no fool, is entrusting her beautiful boy with me, a mere street character so far as she knows.

Or, maybe she sees something else in me, I won't hazard any egotistical answers to that.

And, so I comply with her request. Yes, I will accompany her nephew to St. Patrick's. We'll venture back out into the miserable weather. Seems my lot in life right now anyway so why resist. Mitch meets my eyes with his and a slight look of appreciation mixed with a certain wry resignation flows across his face like a passing soft light. This is a wry fellow, that's the best description I can give you. He is finding his transcendence via transgression. A certain personal quest for an authenticity to his life, the experience of action no matter the little risks involved. I know him well enough because perhaps I see some of me in him. (My mother once told me that any soldier who is willing to kill is willing to be killed. It's all about the risking providing sufficient intensity in experience. In the intensity is the authenticity.)

Mitch and I hike up our hoodies and march out the door into the cold wind and rain. I immediately regret my decision, having become a complete wuss about bad weather. Overexposure and the like,

I suppose. Mitchell, however, strides into it seemingly oblivious or maybe just accepting it as one more difficulty to be marched through to wherever he's going.

Along the way Mitch stops and asks me to go into the Shell gas station convenience store and buy him a pack of smokes. I momentarily hesitate, being a father and all and naturally resistant to aiding and abetting stinking habits among the young. But, also recognizing this young man as much more, the old soul after all, I say, sure why not and turn to enter the store for a pack of cigarettes. It suddenly strikes me that I've just been dumped. Duped into turning my back long enough for this scallywag to abandon me and run off to some nefarious endeavor. I turn and with much relief see Mitch dutifully standing there, in the wind and rain, waiting, stoic, accepting. We join back up and continue the block or so walk to St. Patrick's. He is bold and calm enough to inform me that he is going to try to find an AA meeting there. I am again surprised, (this kid has surprised me a bunch of times in the space of about forty-five minutes. I can't be THAT naïve.) I'm also proud of him, this boy-man I hardly know yet somehow recognize. Maybe he's like some young soldier I once trained, who knows?

As we walk, Mitch's young stride takes him ahead of me one or two paces. His posture has changed to a little more hunched down yet not beaten down, I know that last look, having also affected it on occasion myself. No, this is something else and I am immediately dumbstruck and a little frightened by what thought crosses my already enshrouded mind.

This boy-man, this old soul, is more spirit than body. Every situational awareness alarm in my experienced psyche goes off screaming alert.

He has more than moved away from me physically, Mitch is in another place entirely, only his existence is perceived but most certainly not his essence. I am going too far here, I say to myself. I'm ransacking the common experience to find some ultra-meaning. I am saluting insurgency where it may not really exist. Still, this over-feeling persists, insists to make itself known to me. Scarcely a half-block has been traversed during all of it.

Sudden sadness and resignation comes upon me. Oh you bastard, my old greasy-gray shroud of the spirit has enveloped me powerfully. I am lost in my own thoughts, as this spirit-person Sharon calls Mitchell floats before me. Are his feet really touching the ground? Is this a trick of the light on the rain-slicked concrete sidewalk?

I am suddenly proud, joyful to me in his presence. Punkass little boy, why should I be proud to be with you? You're a mere cog on the great wheel of life, I'm a former prince of the city, a former master of combat arts and servant of the great demi-god Azazel, Lord of war and female beauty. Former this, former that. Then it strikes me like I'm the idiot child of the bunch just getting the point and it comes as nothing less than revelation.

I am but a minor disciple to this spirit man in front of me. He is more than an old soul. He is The Ancient. For him this is but a sojourn upon the earth, in our world and but for a short time. I am crushed in my chest, can hardly breathe, it's freezing out here but my body temperature is sweltering.

I will stop here now, I say to Mitchell. He stops, turns and grants me his wry, small smile. Nods with a monk-like casual bow. Turns and walks away.

I am saddened. Both by his no longer being in my presence and by the grief filled and joy filled knowledge that wherever Mitch is going, I cannot go with him. No one can.

The spirit-boy Mitchell continues on. Walking on to his own, very personal, Golgotha.

As I sit here on this cold, rainy day at table number three in the Fine Arts department of Central Library, I find that this article is too personal and irrelevant to sell to Jay for inclusion in *Whats Up* magazine. Who the eff cares what happens among family members, that's their own deal. Also, I feel that I may have gone too far here in my appraisals of this morning's events. It's too "out there", too weird and if there's one thing I need to avoid it's appearing weird. It would be too clichéd.

And, then, of course, there's Mitchell's feelings and Sharon's trust, neither of which I want to
endanger by my mere ramblings and musings on so
personal a subject. Could I piss-off Mitch by having
this published in the magazine? I don't know.

If he reads this, I think Mitchell will just stop
and slowly turn to grace me with that small, wry
smile as the glow of some passing light crosses his
face.

*

Puncture Palace

Ω

Her dark, powerfully built form moved with effortless grace, seeming to glide rather than stride across the cold floor. A small shiver ran down my spine. I caught the glint of her eyes, professional, without empathy. Surely, this creature was one of those we have all heard and read about, some storied being of the supernatural other world.

In her grasp she held the viscous-looking tools of her bloody trade. I tensed as she approached and wondered aghast at how others here with me this bleak morning do call her name, worshipfully, beseechingly.

Her authority looms before me. I do not, can not, flinch as she sets about her peculiar handiwork. Oh, Queen of the Sanguine Arts, have mercy on my fragile, mortal being! Spare me the pain, the heart-racing anguish of watching my precious juices pump, pump, pump out of my prostrate body. Resigned to my inescapable fate, I relax as the Dark Queen punctures my vein and commences her unsavory task. Perhaps, in my sacrifice, another creature may yet thrive, live to see another moment in this fleeting life.

After all, that's what so-called "blood banks" or plasma donation centers are all about. *(What? You thought this was some Anne Rice vampire novel?)*

For fifteen or twenty bucks, such "donation" centers will pay you for the plasma portion of your blood. The real stuff that's left over is recycled back into you. Otherwise, your body would be like a car engine that's two quarts low on oil. Ungood. This way, the useful, transferable stuff, ("stuff" being the actual, technical, scientific term...,) is screened, processed and used by other humans in need of, to use the precise term, stuff. This is a good thing. Also, getting a small stipend to fund my next beer outing is a nice touch. Oh, wait. I'm just kidding, you know. For the shock value of such an outlandish assertion. Really. Beer? What beer?

To those for whom this whole blood-letting adventure/mini-treasure hunt appeals, there are certain insider tips to be realized. First, it is important to arrive early. I don't mean after breakfast and watching morning TV drivel. I mean 5:30 AM. Okay, 6 AM if you don't mind being number ten in line. Anyone so foolhardy as to arrive when the blood-joint actually opens, say around 7 AM, is in for a rude surprise. No matter what the season it is when you get there, it will be the next season by the time you depart. Late arrivals can fully expect a many-hour ordeal of sitting around a crowded, suffocating and not completely sociable waiting room watching, (it never fails,) the one and only movie you've ever seen on cable. This is purposefully and evilly arranged to numb your senses to the point where your anxiety about the impending discomfort and whooshing fluid is minimized. Well, reduced some.

The process commences with a brief question session by a technician regarding the following concerns: your medical history, present health, sexual habits, least favorite cousin, who you voted for in the last election, a request to please utilize mouthwash next time, and other oh-so-relevant inquiries. You will then be instructed to, *(a)* return to the holding pen with the rest of the chattel, or *(b)* be deemed dangerous to God and all His holy creation, be they animal, mineral or vegetable and brusquely ordered to immediately depart the premises through the door marked "Unclean". Such orders are enforced by the type of security guards who lost their previous jobs when the stalwarts of the Soviet Union went out of business.

Assuming one is included in the (a) group, you may now look forward to about an hour of the aforementioned cable movie torture session followed by the actual puncturing of a vein in your arm and 40 minutes or so of plasma pumping entertainment. So, enjoy!

Oh, and during all of this, the same cable movie will be droning on nearby. The guaranteed mentally and spiritually stupefying effects serve to lessen your comprehension/memory/ability to give legal testimony later should anything untoward occur, say, the technician missing the vein and severing a nerve. That sort of thing.

Despite all of this, there appear to be quite a large number of regulars who utilize the donor clinic. These are primarily the folks who are more accomplished liars, (see previous questioning session,) or, during a previous visit, did not end up donating a container of plasma so polluted with assorted noxious monstrosities that they were banned for life. However long that may be in their case. This is deemed a terrible faux pas, much like trying to leave St. Louis without first *ooohing* and *aahhhing* at the Arch. Try breaking any of these codes and armed troops will turn you back at the stateline.

Upon completion of your donation, a lab assistant will remove the apparatus and then you trade your bottle of precious bodily fluids, *aka* plasma, at the counter where you receive a check for fifteen bucks which the Syrian guys who run the local bodega will cash for you, minus a fee of about three dollars.

As you exit the clinic with gleeful anticipation of which local tavern you'll spend your insultingly small stipend in, be thankful you answered all of the initial questions correctly. And, didn't, um, die on the table.

But, remember next time you want to trade your blood for bucks and the lab girl asks if you ever watch *"Buffy the Vampire Slayer"*, just smile demurely and answer, *"Buffy who?"*

SIDEBAR:

The amount you receive for donating your plasma depends on how frequently you donate and your personal comprehension of Oriental Mathematics and, possibly, the inner workings of the Kabala. I perceive the overall system is rife with unfairness but, then it wouldn't be a system were it otherwise, would it?

Consider this: A one-hundred pound female with an exceedingly common blood type gets about 15 bucks for donating a Dixie cup's worth of plasma. Because she is small, they can't draw a lot from her. But, and this is where the inequities arise, a two-hundred pound male with a very uncommon blood type also receives about 15 bucks, but has to donate a container of his rare vein-squeezin's the size of a Quaker State oil drum. Rarer stuff, plus a huge quantity should equate to more dollars paid by the receiving clinic. Seems logical but what's logic got to do with capitalism, pilgrim?

Other states pay way more. California, for instance, pays an average stipend of forty dollars. Rarer blood-types can garner seventy-five to one-hundred dollars! I am certain our local system somehow violates fair trade practices, various sections of the Geneva Accord and all things just and holy and somewhere in the Bible.

Conclusion: The dollar amounts paid are way too little. After all, it's not like they want your blood or something. Oh, wait, yes they do.

Shortly after this feature appeared in Whats Up magazine, the local clinic closed. We're certain this article had absolutely nothing to do with that. That's our story and, by God, we're stickin' to it.

*

A Place in the Sun

Ω

The gala floats of the annual Mardi Gras parade wind their way down Seventh Street, passed Busch Stadium, eventually into the Soulard neighborhood south of downtown. Tens of thousands of giddy revelers throng the sidewalks and parking lots of ear libation stations. On the riverside of South Seventh, a sprawling, modern, commercial-industrial labyrinth. On the Market side, the oldest, continuously viable neighborhood in the City of St. Louis, the venerable Soulard. But, unbeknownst to the parade-goers, bead-mongers and beer slingers, lurk scores of ghosts. They are the shadows of former boarding houses and rooming houses long closed and torn down. Always a working class community, the Soulard and immediate environs once played host to thousands of single persons living on the economic and social margins of this Midwest industrial burg. Temporary laborers, the unemployed or underemployed, wanderers and vagabonds all made heavy use of the only places in town that offered cheap and easily accessible accommodations.

At their peak of proliferation, it is estimated that nearly sixty rooming houses thrived in the area with hundreds scattered elsewhere throughout the city. Today, most rooming houses are located on the northside of the city, some operating on the sly under the radar of licensing officials. Other large SRO's, (single room occupancy) buildings such as the Mark Twain Hotel downtown, the Lincoln Hotel in mid-town and the Salvation Army's restrictive Railton Residence represent the last of a once common housing option for the city's poorer residents.

Never popular in the estimation of the common citizenry and socially-connected, rooming houses, (those providing space only,) and boarding houses, (those providing both space and meals,) and SRO hotels have purposefully been driven out of business, out-zoned, bulldozed for "urban renewal" and otherwise hounded to virtual extinction. At the same time, the need for affordable accommodations on a more-or-less temporary basis has never been greater. Only during the 1920's and the Great Depression has the demand been so pronounced.

The first barrier to this type of affordable housing takes the form of fear. These fears influence legislation regarding the language of zoning regulations and seemingly heartless decisions by elected officials, thereby creating barriers to the establishment of boarding houses in large, existing buildings or the construction of new ones. The physical layouts of large, older houses and surrounding infrastructure arguments compound the problem. Nobody wants to mess with the inherent problems associated with "permanent transients," being primarily up-ticks in local crime, drug and alcohol abuse and the perceived lowering of real estate values. However, in point of fact, none of these things occurred near the flagship of SRO's in St. Louis, the aforementioned Mark Twain Hotel. This facility is a standing argument for the increased existence of the SRO model for temporarily employed people.

The nationally acclaimed Linderman Creek new-build project also proves that, when managed properly, SRO's can blend into existing neighbor-hoods without depleting values. Up to and through-out the 1920's, many families took in boarders, with the "landlady" acting as surrogate parent or head of household wielding supreme authority over social life, the guests permitted and, even, curfews. To those birds of passage lucky enough to land in such a home, life was considerably improved. At least, for the duration of their stay. Boarding houses provide places of temporary refuge for often vulnerable human vessels. The alternative is the wholly unsatis-factory and perfunctory services provided by the limited "emergency" shelters whose lobbies and doorways may be just another hell-gate to social unrest and personal violence. They exist primarily to sort-of manage a seeming uber-abundance of vaga-bonds in a living theatre of slapstick tragedy. Such meager bunk space facilities are the very metaphoric epitome of the transitory nature of existence itself. Rather than helping the social fabric stay well-knit, they represent its continuing fraying edges.

Curiously, the professional social services industry has grown as the rooming house option has disintegrated. Rather than serve as the only housing option for the homeless, a better mission purpose would be to catch those crying "Olly Olly oxen free!" on their way to a better solution such as the SRO hotel. Today, emergency shelters deal with those broken souls still suffering the spasms of nostalgic pain, slowly being massaged away by denial, isolation and, often, self-medication in the forms of drug and alcohol abuse. They, too, have usually bought into the judgments of society at-large who deem these classic outcasts struggling with poverty, instabilities both mental and physical as the indicators, the telling signs and alert warnings of the existence of personal, moral failure. In other words, stigmatizing and further degrading whatever self-esteem exists by equating poverty and the experience of being homeless with not just a financial situation but rather a critical flaw in character. We can see how this has all changed so dramatically for the worse since the early part of the twentieth-century when little, old ladies rented their spare rooms to wandering souls.

Today, some modern downtown hotel rooms offer unsupervised, individual freedom, a cosmopolitan mixture of neighbors, diverse area services, mobility via the public transportation system and easy walking distances, and so forth. However, this seemingly unfettered existence also creates cultural and social anxiety in the loosening of domestic connections often deemed essential for the maintaining of good "moral order."

Thus, in the economic and social limbo, a certain living Sheol, of the SRO, normal society views such facilities as the potential epicenter of moral depravity. Being poor isn't the crime here, it's that poverty serves as an indicator of personal shortcomings. Such attitudes are helped by the marginalized themselves who persist in delusional thinking, anti-social behavior or seek solace in the open consumption of drugs and alcohol in the vain attempt to gain relief from the cruel efficiencies of reality.

All transients, then, live in a pervasive gray cloud of suspicions both warranted and not, depending on the individual involved. Therein lies the rub. Individual circumstances and character are almost never figured into the equation. Conventional wisdom professed that SROs and boarding houses uniformly attracted and housed the "undesirable" persons of society and, therefore, must be located, um, elsewhere, if allowed to exist at all.

Remember the Soulard neighborhood we visited earlier in our sad tale? Over four hundred residences were demolished to make way for that commercial-industrial zone along Seventh Street. Within those very neighborhoods stood many rooming houses providing working folks dignified if basic accommodation. Nobody but the most bold would claim to this day that a large part of that urban renewal demolition was specifically designed to eliminate once and for all the very existence or possibility of temporary lodgings.

Carved into some of the moldings of the Lincoln Hotel and in the window sills of the New

Life Evangelistic Center, (a vermin-infested hellhole that also serves as an emergency men's shelter,) are people's initials, names and dates, presumably of former transient residents. No one has really attempted to remove those scratchings, perhaps because these pitiful scratchings are someone's claim to have ever existed at all, to have incarnated someplace, a heartrending bid for some kind of acknowledgement of their being, existence, even immortality. The empty nest left by a long gone sparrow, its lingering souvenir of mortal being.

Where once thousands of rooming houses and transient hotels sprouted all around the nation to house the unemployed or working poor, today they barely exist anywhere, at all. Yet, last year, a record-setting number of people were laid-off from their jobs. Not all would lose their homes, of course, but too many have. The difference today being, they have nowhere else to go.

The transient nature of life in an old, industrial city like St. Louis is exemplified as the whole region seems to slope towards and converge on the fast-flowing, mighty Mississippi River. Things here flow on, including people and their meager lives. The river is a point along and towards which all major and idealized sites of this city converge. To look far downstream is to see its visual vanishing point. Rooming houses of the city are the social vanishing points for the marginalized that, like this river, eventually flow downstream, seemingly unstoppable, to inevitably disappear on the far horizons of life.

Alas, like the waters of the great river, more wanderers flow in and pass us by on their own life journeys, ever flowing on the human tide of a tragedy nearly triumphant.

Could you stop and rest awhile, stranger?

In this city, the answer will be *"No, not here!"*

*

The Caves

Ω

Not every hobo can tolerate the shelters. Such places are full of thugs, druggies, predators of every stripe and dimension. Shelters can appear as mere in-between points for the general criminal population who will eventually cycle back into jail. For some few solitary souls, there are other places to call home.

A good place to sleep, which is to say, reasonably safe, sheltered from the wind and hard to see by passersby, *aka* the police, is a cherished spot the location of which most hoboes will not share with each other. Occasionally, some spot can accommodate three or four and impromptu allegiances arise for mutual defense and limited time. One of my early personal favorites was the shoulder-wide space between the Locust Street handicap ramp and the wall of the Bishop Tuttle Memorial building. It was hard to spot, sheltered from the main wind and one lovely night I spent covered by a light blanket of snow. It was peaceful, serene, chilly but not cold.

I stopped using it after that one night because the next night some demon-in-training had dumped a huge, stinking pile o-crap in that very location. The fact of it being on church property no doubt gained the creature extra points with his Dark Master. But I digress.

For sheer privacy, defensible space and all things atavistic, nothing beats a good cave. In happens by lucky coincidence that the St. Louis region is honeycombed with scores of caves. It is a natural geological feature that helped our original beer barons settle here. Naturally cool places for beer barrels. Some of the caves were once famous nightclubs, some notorious speakeasies, some the final resting place of those who got in trouble with the mob guys who ran the aforementioned hotspots (or would it be cool spots?) Tales of crimes most foul and legendary hauntings continue to this day.

There are two caves that are best known by the hobo world. I shall reveal them for you now but caution you not to venture in to either of them unless accompanied by a U.S. Marine combat team.

There are other caves I have been in, *(because, hey, I'm crazy like dat...,)* that I will not tell you about because of their excessive weirdness and dangerous structures.

Probably the most famous hobo cave is the one running alongside North Tucker Avenue, just past the Post-Dispatch building. It is actually a former railroad tunnel, long since abandoned. There are denizens of this dark warren that have resided here and made it their own property by virtue of successful combat and pure longevity. The cave is their chance to return to a safer place and time, their mother's womb, although she was probably a crackhead. These are the true hobos, the ones who never seek any help from social services, don't enter churches, won't go near an emergency shelter, would rather walk in terrible weather than board a bus loaded with other people, their spirits long flushed into these sewer-like places. These are catacombs of the living, the disoriented, the dismayed, the discarded. This is where the invisible men live, in half-light of weak candles, protean, devoid of all further illusions or hope. These caves are as impregnable as the underground lairs of the souls inhabiting them. Known only to God and the Devil. The cops won't go there.

The entrance to the Tucker Tunnel is dark. No light entering from the opposite end can be perceived. To venture in even a few steps is to invite immediate attack by box-cutter, club, knife, even the long clawlike nails growing on the hands of half-men half-beasts within. So a couple of fellow adventurers and I go in. Our hardy band is made up of older street guys, all military veterans, all half-nuts for one reason or another. We are armed and think we're ready, thus proving the half-nuts claim.

Nothing happens. At first. Then, we all hear - it. Very low, about fifty feet ahead. Murmurings, anger slowly coming to a full boil. We have entered the sanctuary of some fool who in his arrogance believes this hole in the ground to be exclusively his. Any wise man would leave him to it but none of those guys are here right now. Cautiously but steadily we advance deeper into the darkness.

And then this long-bearded, rail-thin, long-limbed, rather tall wide-eyed creature-man with arms raised above his head takes three or four long strides towards us into the weak light of our one flashlight. (A puny little thing that any normal person would use for, say, sticking a house key in the lock at night.) Then he stops and freezes without changing his facial expression. Evidently nobody has every remained in place after one of his ridiculous feints. His face actually shows surprise and some fear. Then he softens completely. I mean, he transforms into a smiling hale-fellow well-met kinda guy like he's just met some ole' drinking buddies of his. My friend Rex busts out laughing. No doubt as much in relief as amusement. Then this apparition from Conan the Barbarian asks in a conspiratorial tone: *"Are you gentlemen (!) lookin' to check out this cave?"* I immediately note it's now *"this"* cave and not *"my"* cave. This is a good sign. No proprietary sense of ownership about this place means no combat to defend it.

Of course, we cannot resist such a gracious invitation and without hesitation or regard for this weird old guy now take big strides further into the cave.

It's a trap. From both sides, off shelf-like recesses of the cave's walls tumble four, then six more men. All wide-eyed and NOT friendly. I feel that old resignation come over me. The one that says it'll be whatever it'll be, that strange calmness, the disassociation from what I know will be great levels of pain.

Suddenly, our original caveman turns toward the newcomers and waves his arms maniacally, warning them off, settling them down. *"It's okay!"* he bellows and it echoes incredibly even against the dirt sides. Must be the old concrete base for the rail tracks and here and there I spot fragments of what once must have been a concrete reinforcement of some sort. *"These fellas are my friends!"*

Huh? I mean yessir! Robotic like, but not taking their eyes off us until their heads are turned nearly all the way around, the entire tribe turns as one. Together, without another word, we process

91

through the cave. It strikes me so much like a combat squad moving through enemy territory. Don't these guys live here? What are they afraid of? Now, I'm afraid because I just asked myself that last question.

A few yards more and we enter a forest. Not of trees but of discarded hypodermic needles. Like drug addicts use. Under foot I hear and feel the crunch of broken glass, that light shard of the tube and heavier pieces, most likely empty beer bottles and the like. I immediately assume those bottles got broken in a massive bombardment onto the heads of the last bunch of explorers who ventured this way. Some of the needles are sticking straight up out of the wet dirt. Some have been obviously placed to stick out from the side walls. Punji stakes. Seen this trick before. Didn't care for it then, don't much care for it now. Real bad news if you get yourself stuck on this stuff. No amount of free medical attention at St. Patrick's or Grace Hill is gonna save you now, asshole.

The cavemen move with certain grace, slowly turning this way, then that, knowledgeable as to the precise location of each set of defensive spikes. Hey, you're the evil bastards who put this shit in here to begin with. That makes you the drug addicts. And, that changes our whole potential situation here. Just when I figure we're about to make a decision as to jump these guys by surprise and jam our way out here or not, we round a short curve and light floods in from the other end of the tunnel. The last few yards are as free of detritus as the first few yards were. Unless you count the cave men, of course.

We three turn to say farewell to our hosts and are astonished to see that they have already disappeared. One presumes back into the cave but, who knows? Maybe the Mother Ship beamed them up. Maybe the Great Adversary beamed them down. But, whatever, they are just as surely gone, following with certain cunning veracity the imperatives of self-survival.

The second cave I shall now reveal is a far greater construct of nature and incredibly more dangerous. It is also way spookier. The cave, or rather cave system, is located beneath what is now a city park. Once upon a time, it was a pauper's cemetery and that's where the spooky part comes from.

On this expedition, it is again Rex, Bill the Fat German, (his street description to differentiate him from Hairy Bill, a weird guy,) and yours truly. Emboldened by our recent successful foray into and, much more importantly, out of the Tucker Tunnel, we have decided to check out another infamous cave system reputedly populated by a wide and wild array of street characters, although I have never understood why they should be considered street hoboes if they are, in fact, living in caves. Go figure. Anyway, this involves traveling by bus a considerable distance which involves coming up with the bus fare which involves raising some funds which involves me writing another article for Jay's *Whats Up* magazine. So, naturally I con him into fronting the money to me on the proposal that I'll write some article in the future for him, possibly based on our now not-so-secret upcoming cave mission. Whew. Thus, having cleverly obtained a grubstake, off we go.

It is, at once, determined by all present to be an enormous mistake. The first thing that happens upon arriving at the supposed entrance to the big, secret cave is that some local resident starts yelling at us and threatening to call the police. The fact that some of this is yelled in Spanish doesn't aid our immediate grasp of the situation. So, we do what any red-blooded American combat veteran born and raised in the Midwest, former Boy Scouts one and all, would naturally do. We run. Rounding the corner of an obviously very old, boarded-up brick building, Bill ducks down into what looks to me like one of those exterior basement entry things where you lift up a door and climb down steps. He does just exactly that only the last few steps have apparently either rotted away or been taken away to prevent this very incursion from happening. Bill falls into the black hole of...somewhere. He makes no sound. Doesn't cry out. Doesn't even cuss so now I know it's bad. Then, ever so softly, I hear Bill mumble "F—k." Okay, that's good news. That's the spirit, you old, Fat German. We all see our chance to duck the local

95

raving, Spanish-spewing, police-calling lunatic and follow Bill down into his hole. It is, in fact, a basement of sorts. Not deep enough to stand up in but good enough. Hey, it's almost a cave. Trusty Rex fires up a lighter and instantly we see a wood door in the wall of the shallow basement. With our luck, Ceres will be just on the other side. So, naturally, we pry it open.

To our amazement, trepidation and delight it is clearly a cave. A huge, high, deep cavern. There is some kind of structure in it and upon venturing forward we determine it to be a great beer casket, ancient and rotting away. It is wonderfully cool down here. Maybe some other old, Fat German beer brewer knew this about our caves and selected this very one for his storage area. It is so utterly appropriate that Bill found this cave. We all start laughing, somewhat hysterically some might say, overwhelmed with mirth and a sense of accomplishment.

There is nothing to do now but explore the place. Rex immediately begins waxing poetic about how this place could be our new home, we could live here, maybe find a fresh water spring, be sheltered from the weather in all seasons. He's still talking when he steps into a big, eff'n hole about three feet deep. He's definitely twisted or sprained something and he just rolls a little and moans. Damn. Some fine housewarming party this is turning out to be.

That's two out of us three. So far, I'm the only one who hasn't hurt himself. Yet. No sooner does that thought escape my consciousness that I smack my forehead straight into a beam or support on the ceiling. When did this cave shrink? Now, I'm sitting down rubbing my head, Rex is lying there rubbing his ankle or leg or hip or all three and Bill is saying he thinks he cramped his back muscles in the fall. See. This is why old hoboes and other fools should just hang out at the library and look at pretty pictures of other places they'll never actually get to visit.

What started out as a Big Adventure, rapidly turned into a local chase, is now devolving into some hoboized version of the Three Stooges. The Three Damaged Stooges. Something else is wrong here. I can't breathe, at least, not very well. Rex is now just lying there, not moving much. Bill is leaning against the cave wall. I don't feel so good myself. The air. The air is bad somehow, someway. Then it hits me. The acrid stench of something dead. Maybe long dead. I'm hoping it's some animal that crawled in here to die in peace and whose carcass is somewhere more or less nearby. I stand up, unsteady, unsure, disoriented a bit. I take four or five small steps forward. There is something down here. Lots of something.

You're not going to want to hear what we found in that cave. You should not read this report to children. Got it? Savvy?

There are skeletons down here. Scores of them. Human remains of every variety. Very old, been here a real long time. Not as in American Indian old, but rather as in Civil War old. I am completely speechless. Just this side of freaked.

I turn to the other fellas and say in as calm a voice as I can muster, *"Let's go. We don't belong here. We're all beat up. We can come back another time, better prepared."*

In homage to my stellar oratory skills, my perspicacious persuasions, they all readily agree to follow me out of this wretched place, here and now. Or, perhaps because they're all beat to shit and getting all boo-boo kitty-faced. We climb out, survey the terrain for coppers and mad Spaniards, and make good our escape.

Later, back here at Central Library, I read about the old city cemetery for paupers. Most of the victims of a yellow fever epidemic were buried there. After the city decided to make the area a park for the then-new fine houses being built, in the late 1880's, the city contracted with workers to remove the bodies from the cemetery to the Jefferson Barracks/Koch Hospital area. The history books claim they did just that. I can tell you with certain authority, not everybody made it out of there. Some are still back there, thrown down into old beer baron caverns rather than expensively removed and transported.

Three former adventurers, Trusty Rex, Bill the Fat German and Yours Truly know the truth of the matter. Rest in peace, but not forgotten. *Fini.*

Robert E. Lipscomb

Morning of the Gray Wolf

Ω

The long walk from Sunshine Mission men's shelter on North Tucker into the downtown area is fraught with its own, special hazards. In addition to being unceremoniously ushered out of the shelter into the cold, dark, wet or whatever weather, it is always that time of the pre-dawn morning when only truck drivers and cops are moving about the streets. Well, except for that special breed of thundercat punk who, moving in packs, lie in wait for the weak, the distracted by personal miseries, you know, the homeless. By attacking the least valued members of society, these roving squads of hooligans, usually teenagers, know they can hone their close quarters combat skills without fear of reprisal by the law. So, they wait, parked in cars on side streets, for a small group of suitable quarry to flutter by. On this particular morning, I am in such a flock.

This cold, dark morning we stride along, moving through the deserted and dangerous area just north of the city proper, fully aware of potential encounters and praying silently to avoid the same. Unfortunately, I am not accompanied by Trusty Rex, an old soldier who would fight anybody anywhere anytime no matter the odds. No. This morning I have Bill the Fat German, roly-poly, short Johnnie and the retired from life or caring David. In battle, essentially useless. I know this, of course, and try to maintain my pace and posture in a manner evidencing both readiness and ability to handle whatever comes our way. In other words, I'm counting on the bluff to carry us through.

Almost out of the dark stretch, just a half-block from the Post-Dispatch newspaper building, out from the last side street comes our worst alternative. Three young black guys, probably teenager gangstas of some sort, jump out of an old sedan and rush us. I just stop and look at them. The first peels away from me and bowls over Johnnie, who is in constant jeopardy of bowling over on his own. The second goes straight at Bill the Fat German, grabs the strap of his bag and spins him around into the street. A car swerves into the other lane to avoid running him down. I think I hear Bill's head smack the pavement. He sort of half-sits up, then lays back down. The kid who jumped him has deftly slashed open Bill's bag of clothes and junk and greedily, kind of crazily it seems to me, is pulling everything out, looking for something, anything of value. The third guy in starts towards me. I let my backpack slide off my shoulder and take up a fighting stance. It's been a long time since I've had to actually duke it out so I know my body can't take the heat but, right now, right here, I'm an Army sergeant again, I'm sparring with my dad, I'm ready in my heart to create mayhem, damage and destruction. This guy pauses and appraises me for just a moment. The other two pass him by running back to the car. My guy half-smiles, shakes his head and shuffle-jogs back to the car. Then I see the real threat here. The driver has half emerged from the car and is staring dead at me. It dawns on me with no doubt this fellow is armed with something, probably a handgun or one of those eff-d up shotguns cut down for quick use. He slowly drops back into the driver's seat, all the doors slam shut and the car backs away, spinning tires and making all kinds of noise. Not exactly your stealth commandoes, here. Bill is getting up slowly, dazed and confused as to where his bag went. His stuff is strewn all over the wet pavement, some of it run over by cars that never bothered to even slightly slow down. Roly-poly Johnnie, somewhere in the midst of this whole thing, got himself up and ran a block away. Good for him. Bitch coward, thanks for the help. Dave never stopped walking, walked coolly right out of the scrap utterly unscathed. I pick up my backpack, the adrenaline dissipating and me just shaking from it and, I suppose, the sudden rush of cold I feel.

I can only speculate as to why that third attacker stopped and turned away. I suspect my face fully showed my intent to put up a real fight. Maybe I looked real old-school to him or, more likely, just too damn old to eff with. Whatever the case, I am the warrior again, if only for a brief moment. The old Army saw cuts through my mind; *you can play with the puppies, but you mess with an old, gray wolf, you just might get bit.*   *Fini.*

Memorial Day

Ω

Most folks spending inordinate amounts of time of the street have favorite spots to just sit peacefully and contemplate the vagaries of life. One such spot for me is a park bench strategically situated to afford a full view of our local Soldiers Memorial.

The best times to be here are in colder weather or in a slight drizzle of rain. Such weather most fully reminds me of the years I devoted to military duty and the personal misery current servicemen deal with everyday. This place, this Memorial, this weather also serves to keep fully fixed in my wandering mind that certain vision of evil and grief foisted on us by those so intent on serving their own dark masters. The Soldiers Memorial is so powerful in architecture, so laden with iconic statuary, that even the great, greasy-gray shroud of the psyche must hold at the perimeters, neither seeking to nor succeeding in penetrating this fortress of heroism before me.

The light rain has begun to fall, first annoying me, then soothing my heated brow. It is always too warm in St. Louis on Memorial Day. I want to be cold. Perhaps to be more closely in step with those heroic departed.

A woman slowly climbs the many steps up to the entrance arches of the Memorial. At first I think she is merely escaping the brief rain shower but then I gauge the pace of her steps and realize she is oblivious to it. She must be lost in her own thoughts, her own memories, her own obligation on this hallowed day. She trudges into the building, head slightly bowed, weighted down by an internal darkness, a certain resignation. She is here to help herself remember, I suppose, to find some trapping of glory, purpose, meaning to the losses she has endured. She must be just one of many thousands, millions, so searching for that evidence granting meaning to the death of her beloved warrior.

The breeze kicks up a bit, the shower threatens to become a summer squall. The woman disappears into the darkness of the vaulted internal courtyard of the Memorial. The wind seeming to flow as if to propel her inside. Maybe the spirits of the fallen have come around to accompany her in an invisible procession, a ghostly honor guard.

The war in Iraq and elsewhere drags on, like some Manichean struggle between Good and Evil. The Devil's armies are loose upon the world. God is under siege. Such concepts escape my consciousness as quickly as the breeze blows past. Too much, too broad, too meta. What truly matters is this woman, this grief, this aura she carries of finality. Her soldier is not coming back, no matter who wins the wars.

I suddenly jerk my head up, aware now that I have momentarily dozed off or fallen into daydream. I look up just in time to see the small woman, head covered with scarf like emerging from some sacred sanctuary, some Cathedral of War, descend the last of the Memorial's steps and her footsteps, like the raindrops, drum lightly and march away.

I think of the two-hundred thousand military veterans I hear are now experiencing homelessness. I wonder what the ancient Greeks would have done for their returning warriors. I am amazed and enraged that this nation I have trained to defend in the past, and still so love, can abide this dishonor, the ever-present evidence of disrespect to those who have so selflessly served and sacrificed and now wander like some gallant, lost legion in the wilderness. I pray for a new Alexander the Great to lead his ragged army through the desert of the forgotten. I look down the sidewalk and some street guy ambles at the corner. Is he a veteran? Why has his nation forsaken him?

In the distance I hear a marching band warming up their instruments for the annual Memorial Day Parade, a festival honoring our fallen warriors. I begin to weep. I am so thankful the light rain hides the tears slowly rolling down my tired, old face.

*

Afternoon of Fools

Ω

My good friend Angry Dave and I are ensconced upon a great park bench just across from the old Federal building on Market Street. This is a wonderful vantage from which to view and appraise the parade of passing fools alight upon our fair city streets this fine, spring day.

We often come here to munch our lunch, that being a most satisfying repast of microwave burgers and super-gulps from the nearby quick shop. We are blessed to be able to afford such dining splendor due to the fortuitous generosity of Pastor Nancy, in my case, and the Federal government's food stamp card, in Angry Dave's case. How we laugh and laugh at the poor starving beggars wandering in our midst. Fools! This town is full of food and, if you can't find the three places serving free meals, at least, find a generous priest.

We two vagabonds of the day watch with increasing bemusement the physical antics and acting out of several well-known street characters whose task, it appears to be, is to wander up and down the same streets everyday acting all crazy. We love it. Free theater of the absurd. Nothing beats real fools for live entertainment value. *That ain't actin', they actually be like dat.*

First up today is one of the all-time reliable crazies, Devil Boy. Devil Boy earns his moniker on the street for his wide, blazing-red eyes, his low, rumble-grumble voice and constant conversation with his personal entourage of invisible demons. Mumbling rather loudly such things as, *"Shut up, all of ya's!"* and *"Leave me alone or I'll kill you!"* Big fun! This grumbling-rumbling patter goes on continuously, nonstop, all day. One wonders where he gets the breath for it and can pace himself so quickly up and down the sidewalk at the same time. This time, he stops dead in his tracks, like he knows we're watching him. He doesn't turn his head to look at us. Oh, now we see. He has paused to listen to some message from the entourage. He is considering its value and instructive import. He suddenly throw his head back in a great guffaw as he gets the joke he was just told. By the demons. Man, this is too rich. How much would the tickets cost for this show if Fox got a hold it? It's not acting, it's real! We wait patiently for Devil Boy to walk on and then roll out our own laughter, so thankful that God had deemed us worthy to send such mirthful moments. What a great day this is turning out to be!

From down the block, the lunchtime crowd of office workers is parting like the Red Sea. Swirling through their midst is a short, black, stout woman yelling, *"Get outa my way, there's things to be done!"* This, while cart-wheeling her arms round and round. It looks exhausting. Several pedestrians fire up there cells phones, maybe to call the local cop patrol to come and settle this lunatic down. She looks ever so dangerous. I see one guy point his cell phone at her. He must have one of those new, in-phone camera things. What a good friend he must be to share this special moment with his friends. Over and over she shouts her manic mantra. Arms cart-wheeling, carving a path through the stupefied throng. Man, can it get any better than this? Thank you, ACLU for freeing the fools and lunatics back in the '80's! Free street theatre, it's what makes America great. Mere pissing-on-trees, loud, vulgar public drunks can't compare to this. How common, how meager. We gots REAL fools out here now! Thank you, thank you.

Too close behind us, Angry Dave and I hear, feel almost, the rustling of paper. Newspaper, it turns out. Just a few steps away, a very tall, very, very thin "man" of a truly disturbing, gray-ashen complexion, is pulling a discarded newspaper up out of a corner trash barrel, briefly looking at the section in hand and, then, tossing the newspaper onto the ground. He is clearly not focusing on what he is looking at. There is no more comprehension of the content of that paper than the pigeon nearby has. (Although, a pigeon has, indeed, flopped onto a discarded newspaper section lying on the sidewalk and appears to be searching it for something. Probably something to eat, a tiny, tasty cornel of something, maybe reading the Sports section, but who really knows?!?)

Zombie-like, mechanically, unnaturally motioned. Yes, this is a new character for us. We dub him Zombie Man. He is just exactly like those crea- tures from *Night of the Living Dead*. Dave and I make no sound. We do not, as is our habit, yell at Zombie Man to *"Hey, pick up that shit! Don't you see that trash can right in front of you?"* Because, we realize he does not, in fact, have any knowledge of any trashcan or anything else. He's a Zombie! Didn't we already tell you this? Pay attention, for God's sake.

A roving police patrol car comes to a halt at the corner just behind our Zombie Man. A cop rolls down the window and, with an obviously tired-of- this-stuff voice, inquires, *"Hey! We got a problem here, sir?"* Zombie Man half turns to face the cop, slowly turns back to continue his intrepid search in the trashcan for some treasure whatever demon he is possessed by insists he find. The cop engages in a brief consult with the cop driving, rolls up his win- dow, the patrol car slowly moves on. See? The cops enjoy this live theater as much as we do! Maybe.

Anyway, our afternoon of fools is not yet quite over. A bevy of Asian tourists, probably staying at the hotel in Union Station about a block from here, are strolling through our green sanctuary, the required cameras dangling from their slight necks. About thirty feet from our posted position, a hobo is recumbent upon the earth, peaceful in a shroud of filthy blankets, motionless, apparently asleep. A pigeon has taken up the superior position atop this still form. That would be sufficiently comical but, no, it gets even better.

The three Asian tourists suddenly stop, transfixed, amazed by the still-life before them. The girl of the group snatches up her camera and snaps off several shots of this wonderful evidence of America's useless citizenry. Then, one of the male tourists proclaims, *"You lie there all day! Do nothing! NOTHING!"* He can scarcely comprehend it, it angers him. It entertains the hell out of us and we bust out laughing. This is hilarious.

The petite girl moves forward to snap a closer picture of her newly discovered life-form. Just then, the hobo moves, suddenly lifts his head and spies girl with camera. A shot of resigned disgust bursts from his throat. His head lolls back, eyes closing. There is no threat here, just another moron who won't leave him alone. Not his first rodeo, no concern here.

The girl jumps back, shocked at the hobo's sudden movement, like a small child does in the snake room at the Zoo. The tourists make a larger-than-necessary circuit around the once again still-life, looking back protectively, ready to make a run for it if need be.

Angry Dave, just for a little while, isn't angry. We smile the knowing smiles of the world traveler, the cosmopolitan, the street experienced. What a fine day this has been. We give thanks to God for our many blessings.

Just across the street, sitting around the outside terrace of the mostly-vacant Federal Building, some office workers eat their meager lunches. An incredibly fat person in uniform, one of those rent-a-cop types, is staring at Angry Dave and me, hands on hips in the typical stance of the lowly guardian of order, demanding to be noticed, his authority ac-knowledged. It occurs to me he's surveying us, these two white, middle-aged men posted on a park bench directly across from a government building. You can see his mental wheels turning from here, he's wondering if perhaps we are some kind of advance team, scoping out this critical government facility for future terrorist attack. Since 9/11, everyone has apparently lost their eff'n minds. *We grew up here, sir, we are eating lunch, as anyone can plainly see.*

Not wishing to disturb the guard's inner peace, not really relishing his stare, we slowly arise from our bench and amble away to find some more welcoming locale. I give thanks to God for saving this greatest of fools for last.

*

Media Mornings

Ω

Jay Swoboda, along with a small but hardy band of street-hawkers and I have pushed and promoted our intrepid journalistic endeavor, *Whats Up* magazine, for several months now. Even though Jay has obtained and issued the required vendor permits, some of us are continually harassed by roving police patrols. Sometimes one of our guys will be arrested for "aggressive panhandling" or "street demonstration." We have no doubt that some element of truthfulness resides in those charges. We also suspect that some of the money received via the sale of the magazine to passersby is being ultimately diverted to drugs and alcohol. It is evident we can't alter engrained personal behavior patterns of some of our street vendors. But, one thing we can attempt is to raise the awareness level of the general public to the on-going plight of those experiencing homelessness and cycles of poverty. To this end, Jay turns to the local media for help.

One morning, Jay arrives, more or less without warning, at Christ Church Cathedral's "Club Cathedral", our free bagels-and-coffee service for the "downtown neighbors", (a politically correct euphemism for the local hoboes.) He walks up to me and states, like I know what he's talking about, *"Ya ready to go be on the radio?"*

"Uh, no. What?" I reply wittily, ever the sharp, insightful mind that I am at 0-Light Thirty. Not.

It seems that Jay, in his tireless campaign to help the homeless and presumably downtrodden, as well as guys like me out on The Great Adventure to encounter his authentic self, has secured air-time, for free, on a local radio station. The idea is to get the message out there about the plight of the street, generally, and to muster financial and resource support for me, specifically. I instantly, with my steel-trap mental acuity, deduce this a grand opportunity to pump-up the volume regarding my personal cause, possibly to garner enough of the right kind of attention that leads to opportunities heretofore unthinkable.

117

"Okay," I enthuse, *"Let's go!"*

Jay eyes me suspiciously, appraising, probably re-considering the wisdom of calling me in on
this mission. The second-doubting passed, his face
brightens up as we stride off with good cheer in our
hearts and absolutely no idea in our heads what's
coming next.

Motoring over to a high-rise in the Central
West End, we enter a building that is directly next to,
actually part of the same complex, as my old penthouse apartment! I take this as a sign from God. We
enter the ornate lobby, sign in with the doorman,
(thankfully, not anyone I recognize and who, ergo,
doesn't recognize me as a former, honorable occu-
pant of this complex,) board the elevator for a short,
shaky ride to the apartment that is actually used as a
radio station. Kinda cool.

Having never been in a radio studio before, I
have no idea how this strange magic occurs. Lights
and hand gestures from some controller guy behind a
glass window, (is he dangerous?), facial expressions
from the radio host, signaling when to speak and

when to remain utterly silent. At varying breaks, she announces that we are Off Air and can speak openly. I instantly suspect this is a ploy to get us to say something too candid, that we are really still broadcasting. Paranoia being part of the poor man's baggage and, certainly, part of the baggage carried by a former Army sergeant, middle-aged, twice-married-divorced, used-to-be-prosperous white man who has unceremoniously fallen from grace.

Jay speaks eloquently and knowledgably about the issues of those experiencing homelessness. He pleads for understanding and less fear when encountering one of our vendors hawking the magazine. The money goes for a good cause, he reminds us. The radio host is friendly, non-confrontational, appropriately probing but not insufferable by any means. In other words, quite the contrary to what I expected.

Our hour or so of air time concludes. We depart graciously. I am wonderfully energized by this communicating with the world at large, this chance to speak the truth.

Jay thanks me for participating, buys lunch for us, I fob a few bucks off him. The usual generosity of the Jay. He remains singular in his focus, ever steadfast in his willingness to help out. I silently resolve that if ever the opportunity arises in the future when I am able to return the favor to Jay, I will unhesitatingly do so. Paying it forward and all.

Mr. Swoboda is not quite done with the media, it turns out. He has contacted and convinced a reporter from the *Post-Dispatch* newspaper to grant us a feature column and send a photographer to one of my better *Whats Up* magazine sales spots, Keiner Plaza, at lunchtime. Although I am primarily earning my walk-around money by writing articles for the magazine and other tiny, pickup freelance gigs, I still occasionally sally forth with a bundle of magazines under arm to extol the virtues of the struggling underclass, purvey the insights of our journalistic endeavor and otherwise extract vast gobs of cash from passersby. I neglect to mention to anyone that I used to be a member of the Republican National Committee, donating sufficient sums to the GOP, making like a loyal, Danforth-style Republican. Big fun, once upon a time. Not so much, right now.

Jay and I arrive at the appointed hour, blessed by a wonderfully clear, sunny lunch hour. The newspaper photographer is floating around trying to be unobtrusive to the natural order of events. This cannot be a staged thing. *"We only shoot what's real."* intones the photographer. The action begins.

A strongish, fortyish, blonde business woman emerges from the hotel across the street, quick-steps across Market Street and enters my domain. ("Killing ground" might be too melodramatic a term...) She spots me, I see her see me, the encounter ensues. I state my brief case, holding the magazine up for her to see the cover and catch an idea of what this is all about. She stops, staring at the cover, clearly reading it, taking it in. She decides. Reaching into her purse she pulls out a great gob of cash, ones I can tell, thrusting out her arm stiffly, commanding, *"Here, take this. Good luck."* There is the hint of a foreign accent, probably Dutch, possibly German. Having served a few years with the Army stationed in Germany, my ear is attuned to the dialect. I thank her profusely but not obsequiously, she strides away, head slightly bowed as if in thoughtful consideration of this unexpected occurrence in her routine. The newspaper photographer is furiously firing away with her way-too-elaborate camera. Does she realize that a goodly proportion of the street characters wandering around this area would forcefully relieve her of that device if given half a chance? I decide not to tell her this particular opinion, given that we're out here trying to help those very same street thugs, I mean, characters.

Anyway, next up, I am delighted to see, is a pair of Asian girls, probably college students. I cannot help but recall my recent observation of another Asian group's reaction to encountering a recumbent hobo in their path. My smile is so big they immediately return it, not realizing the source of my bemused expression.

I trot out my tried and true patter. They gleefully reach for a few bucks and hand it to me. That very moment in the exchange is captured by the photographer. By cropping to the meeting of our figure tips, it is utterly like the painting on the Sistine Chapel of God and Man touching, reaching out for each other. A common moment between some people meeting on the street is thus captured and published as iconic art.

We all decide that it can't get any better than this. Besides, the lunchtime crowd is waning and I am fatiguing of the exercise of asking anyone for anything. It may enrich my wallet but it degrades my spirit, my already slight sense of self-esteem. The really sustaining and supportive element being the kind responses of the people I have met this day.

The newspaper publishes a huge feature on *Whats Up* magazine, quoting Jay and proclaiming our cause throughout the land. Some pieces of the article focus on yours truly, not necessarily in a complimentary light but certainly in a truthful-enough manner to, I believe, evoke generous response and action in well-off types reading it. Days, then weeks, pass. Nothing happens. Nobody seeks me out to "save me" from the street. I am discouraged but not surprised. What's left to surprise me? I took the shot, hung it all out there, dirty linen and all, in a great bid to raise the consciousness and action of the people. I did not succeed. Add it to a long list.

The magazine struggles on. A few kind hearts send Jay small donations to keep the publication alive. Christ Church Cathedral buys a couple of institutional ads with funds they probably can ill spare. The size and depth of the problems we have illuminated are too massive for even the powerful media to overwhelm.

We are grateful, nevertheless. We soldier on.

*

Carol Meets The Devil

Ω

Christ Church Cathedral's *"Club Cathedral"* morning breakfast program is motoring right along. Having long outgrown the original hallway donuts-and-coffee mayhem, it gained a new, expanded mayhem. Now positioned in a too-small room and the open hallways of the administration building known as the Bishop Tuttle Memorial, where once only a dozen or so gathered, now the building's great, red doors open to a couple of hundred miserable, wandering souls seeking sanctuary and sustenance. If only for a little while, thank you very much.

I come here nearly every morning. Our usual path from the shelter or from wherever we happened to land overnight, is to make the long march to Union Station. Union Station is always open, the toilets many and the guards understanding. There, we freshen up, change clothes, whatever. If we have a couple of bucks, we'll buy a big cup of hot coffee at the American Diner. If one of us has earned some extra dollars working a street festival or, in my case, a writing gig, we'll splurge for the good stuff at Star-buck's. Caffeine is my drug of choice. From Union Station, we'll march back to the Cathedral for the opening of their great doors and Club Cathedral. This may seem on the surface like an appalling waste of time but, one must grasp the fact of street life. Upon arising in the dark of the morn, there is no place to go. No office, no factory, no shop. There is, of course, no home to nest in. There is no nutritional encour-agement of breakfast. Nothing. Save rough weather and rougher glances to struggle through.

So it is that we trudge to the Cathedral for sanctuary, sustenance and, if I am lucky, solace. The latter can be gained by pleasant repartee with the volunteers of the church program and their em-ployed professionals. I eagerly anticipate the days when that one church volunteer named Sharon is present, although it's usually only once a week. Her cheerful demeanor, street-savvy advice and, I don't know what to call it, her spirit glows with something wonderful. Maybe even holy. It's a church, after all, didn't I tell you already?

Anyway, talking to Sharon, or the bookstore lady Jane or her husband Rod, (whom I intrepidly attempt to intercept whenever he alights from the elevator, hot pastries of the chocolate variety on his tray,) and others helps keep my brain alive. If I happen to score both chocolate and coffee, my day is as good as made. Praise be to God and all his mighty angels. Some of whom work here. I think it's the ones with the chocolate!

Anyway, the boss of this bedlam is a guy by the name of Tom Burnham. He's a rather interesting sort, strives to be a real individual character, if somewhat obviously at times. Sporting a Santa Claus length white beard, ponytail and, often, hiking shorts in the bitter cold of winter, this guy has been involved with all-things-homeless and rendering of services to same for at least a decade. It is Tom that I most often gain opportunity for conversation; receive advice and tips regarding life on the street. I call these encounters "talking to grown-ups." I relish, and my mind is kept alive by, the practice of conversation. One of the main topics Tom loves to broach is that about jazz and blues, the music and musicians.

I have listened with varying degrees of care and attention to Mr. Burnham's extensive recitation of the history of Blues, the personalities and life stories of the musicians and what it is all about. It takes month upon month of such conversations for the gist of what Tom is trying to convey to finally begin to sink into the mind of this most dense of God's foolish children, yours truly.

It hasn't really been about which St. Louis jazz or blues master did what. It's been about the metaphor that is the blues. Tom has been trying to help me by putting my miserable life experience in the light of what the blues is saying. What it means. Ah, an attempt to place meaning back into my life. I see your wily ways now, Mr. Tom. Maybe you mean how blues is all about masterful improvisation, about the transcendence of alienation via mighty fine riffin'...How all life, especially that of the struggling, is about picking up the beats and hearing the place *between* the beats in the rhythm of normal life. That's where I'm living now, between the beats in the rhythm of the city. But, knowing what the rhythm is, the beats, the spaces and all, tells me what song I need to hear. The one in my heart. What is the song I sing to myself silently? Is it of rage, frustration, fight, flight, fear and, yes, thanksgiving? Why do all blues masters sing even in the midst of their own often very troubled lives? Oh, I think I'm beginning to get it now, if just one stanza at a time. Verse by verse, the song becomes known to me. This is what I came out onto the streets for, this the lessons of the wilderness. To hear the internal blues and learn to dance anti-strophe with my own demons. Blues proclaim the art of triumph over trials. To raise a voice, to stake one's talent of spirit against the world. Improvise, Bob, improvise. *Sing a new song of triumph, even in the midst of tribulation.* The words won't be happy words. That's not the point. The point is the singing of it.

It will not be long before that philosophy is put to the maximum test.

Recall that earlier I spoke of the very first person I met here at Christ Church Cathedral.

She was the church lady who stormed down the hallway of this building and commanded the boisterous crowd at the donut hand-out to be still. Which they obeyed. Her name was Carol Bledsoe, although I only knew her by that name which I heard the black hoboes address her: Miss Carol. Carol patiently complied with my imprecations to supply me with a simple, yellow writing pad or a cheap ink pen. She also was ready, willing and able to grant me a bit of cogent advice, if she felt so compelled. The latter always delivered with a certain friendliness, like a friend giving another friend timely advice, if that friend seemed to be sailing off-tack. Both her generosity and her insight were much appreciated and I gratefully added her to my inner circle for talking with grown-ups time.

During the Club Cathedral mornings, in the initial days of the service program, anybody and everybody off the street came in. Later, the more obvious thugs and dangerous lunatics were sorted out and more-or-less banned. It was just too disruptive in such a confined area to allow egregiously unsocial behavior, placing everyone in jeopardy. From time to time, I would pass comment to Tom or one of the volunteers about such persons, if I recognized them from the street, having witnessed occasion of madness most dangerous and foul. Sometimes this advice was accepted, sometimes not so much. One such lumbering thug from the street particularly set my internal situational awareness alarms on full howl. I communicated my fear and misgivings about this person to those running the morning program and quickly forgot about it.

Some weeks later, I am sitting at my favorite table in the Fine Arts section of the Central Library downtown, reading yet another book of some sort. (Over the course of my sojourn on the street I probably read all or most of over two hundred books. Words mean things. Reading, writing, talking to grown-ups... can you see a plan here?) I glance up to see who has entered the area, I always quick-appraise anyone entering my space for any potential threat. Can't help myself. Fortunately, I've learned to quit growling a wolfish warning. Just kidding. I never actually growled. I think. Anyway, who do I see but my beloved friend and benefactor of the written word Mr. Jay Swoboda hisself. He doesn't look happy but he does look relieved to have found me. Like that's so difficult. The library's practically ready to place an engraved name plague on this table. *Here sits the Mystic Hobo, all art and artifice. Abandon hope all ye who bother me.* Whatever.

Jay slides into the chair opposite me at the table and fixes me with his *listen to me closely* look. I grant undivided attention.

Jay slowly drops the bomb. *"Someone at the Cathedral has been attacked."*

I respond, not entirely surprised, *"Oh, who?"*

I'm guessing to myself it's Tom Burnham, jumped by one of those lunatics he previously banned from the morning breakfast program.

"Carol Bledsoe, the church secretary." Jay reports and sucks in his breath awaiting my response.

Huh? My face betrays momentary confusion.

Jay states quietly, *"She's dead."*

I cannot grasp it. Carol? My Carol? The gal who grants me paper, pen and patience? That Carol? My mind grinds it down, takes hold of it. The wolf within rises up, all shackles and bared teeth. Now I'm growling, *"Who? Where is he now?"* It is a demand for positive identity. *Number not the enemy*, said Alexander the Great, *simply tell me where they may be found.*

I find myself suddenly and surprisingly on my feet, standing tall and physically coursing with adrenaline, energy, power. I can barely keep from butt-sliding over this table to land the other side and gain the exit from this building. Her killer is loose upon the street, we will seek him, find him, murder his demon ass right here, right now. No questions asked and damned the consequences. Jay holds his hand to my chest.

"The cops are everywhere looking for him. They think they know who it is."

Just then, stern-faced men in ballistic vests enter the library, hands on pistol grips, ready for action.

They quickly stride throughout the library, a likely sanctuary for anyone escaping misdeeds committed just across the street in the Cathedral. Their sudden presence settles me somewhat. I sit back down. It's out of our hands. It was never in our hands. Jay gets up and goes to his next necessary appointments, working for a real living and such.

I quietly close the book before me. I wish now I could remember what title it was. I gather up my backpack and slide the backstraps over my shoulders. I am sore, drained, muscles sapped of the previous adrenaline. I must have flexed every muscle and sinew I have, steeling myself for certain physical combat. The chair slides quietly back under the desk, I walk unsteadily out of the building.

It occurs to me that, in my wanderings, I might accidentally encounter the evil demon who has apparently snuffed out the life of one of God's servants. This is indeed the war I always knew would come. The Devil versus God. The Devil's armies are loosed and God is under siege, even in His own house. It slowly rises up within me that this cannot stand, this is not acceptable.

After all the misery I have suffered, all the foul weather, the disrespect, the loss of self, the giving away of self for that matter, the search to encounter the authentic me somewhere sometime somehow, it all comes down to this stunning moment. I know who I am. I know what I am. *I have always known.*

I am a warrior. I am a man of God. This time, my words will be my weapons, I demand the name of the demon and he shirks from me in fear. Azaz, that god of war and painted beauty, Mammon that god of greed, stand aside. You bore me. Michael is my Captain, Christ is my King.

Everything within me sings the blues, in this terrible, eye-opening moment, how can it be otherwise? I exit the library and immediately set steady stride, purposeful, seeking. To encounter Carol's killer now can only end in one way. His death, my vengeance, no matter the consequences.

Up ahead there is a great commotion. A bevy of cops have swarmed onto some crouching hobo like flies on a shit-pile. Seen this before but, wait, something is different this time. I see them now, scuffling and cuffing, this big demon and the cops. They have him now. He is thrown into a police vehicle.

Air escapes my lungs, no, my entire being deflates. It is past. The inevitable moment of furious hate-filled combat is not to happen now. Why am I here in this place? Futile? Useless? The optional cipher?

I sit wearily, drop really, onto the concrete bench-like extension on the side of the library building. What has happened here? I need to understand it fully, to make use of it. To learn. That is, after all, why I'm out here in the first place. To learn whatever the wilderness might teach me.

*

Susan's Morning

Ω

Carol's suspected killer has been duly captured. What we cannot capture on this morning
following is that old sense of peaceful faith that
everything will be safe enough around here, that
nothing really bad will happen. That sense of security
is gone. Forever.

I walk into the hallway used for the morning
breakfast program, "Club Cathedral." Scarcely a soul
is in the place. This is unusual but to be expected, I
guess. Many of the street people are afraid to enter
here. They believe they will be judged as equal to
Carol's killer. A couple of stalwart volunteers, clearly
must be the true servants of God's work, are here. I
see my friend Sharon and with her a baby in a
stroller! Obviously not the child of such a woman of a
certain age but rather a grandchild, I marvel at the
balls it must take to bring a babe into this place of
recent death.

Soon, one of the Cathedral's priests arrives.
She is Canon Susan Nanny and she seems to have no

real idea what to do now, here, in this place, under these circumstances. I listen to the quiet conversation between Canon Susan and Sharon and learn that the leaders of the Cathedral have ordered the morning breakfast program closed down, pending review. This makes sense on an emotional level; their fears are justified even though the person who allegedly killed Carol did so well into the afternoon, long after the morning program had closed. He is a known lunatic in this area, occasionally entering the sanctuary and getting into arguments with the statues of the saints carved in the Reredo. The killer is also, as it happens, one of the persons I raised the warning flags about weeks ago, such advice obviously falling on deaf ears or the earshot of those who routinely disregard the advice of mere street folks, like me.

A few street folks straggle in, downtrodden, sheepish. Embarrassed. Yesterday afternoon, as word of Carol's death spread, I witnessed hard-core, tough-guy street characters break down in tears and sobbing upon learning it was *their Miss Carol.* A couple of those are in here, now. Silent. Sick. Lost more than ever.

Canon Susan is making about the room used for dispensing bagels and coffee with the help of my friend Sharon. Susan is shaky. She is making a good show of holding herself together but this is too much, Carol's murder is too much. Even for a priest. They deal with death professionally, you know. In spite of Susan's obviously unnerved and grief-ridden state, she stands here, holding the banner, as it were. She refuses to be bowed before the Great Adversary. Maybe she believes as I do that the Devil Himself had to invade this holy place, this sacred ground, and try to stop the works being done here, simply because of the great glory to God each and every morning proclaimed as His servants went about ministering to these, the least of His children. Here, in this morning that shall forever be remembered by me as "Susan's morning", Canon Nanny stands shaken but not bowed. Afraid but not in flight. Her courage is palpable.

This morning, I realize yet another, inescapably important fact of my life. This is my church. I have found a new faith family I respect. I believe they are the real deal. This Cathedral will serve as my sanctuary also. Its strength will be my strength, its courage, as I see so clearly evidenced before me, will be part of my courage. To stand against whatever this life brings and nonetheless proclaim through presence and works the glory of my God, the one and true, high holy king. The Devil be damned. Here in this mighty fortress of the Holy Spirit, in this mysterious church in the middle of the city, here at Christ Church Cathedral, The Devil Himself has done his damnedest and gone down to utter defeat.

Upon the adversary's chest the small foot of a little priest woman named Susan Nanny is firmly planted and she ain't about to let him get up and ruin this work. Not here. Not this morning. This is Susan's morning.

*

A Letter to Carol

Ω

This article originally appeared in Whats Up magazine,

on behalf of the clients of Christ Church Cathedral's

"Club Cathedral", the morning breakfast program for

the area's homeless. Not given to publishing features

obviously pertaining to matters in religious institutions,

(that wasn't our beat, as journalists say,) a major

exception to the rule was made in this instance.

Dear Carol:

Just a brief note of thanks for all your consid-
erations, none deemed small by me and too numerous to recall in this moment. Also, thank you for your
generosity of spirit, which provided me the emotional uplift, the practical perspectives of your always
reality-based understanding, in order that I may face
yet another day being homeless, but not without
hope and broke, but only financially so.

Early on, upon being cast out on this sea of
constant anxiety and creeping despair, you tossed me
a tether-line to normalcy, higher thinking and friend-

ship. Being broke, this became my new wealth. Being homeless, the church became my citadel. For all intents and purposes, you, Carol, are the church. From our almost daily conversations, you know that I was raised in a faith-filled community. My parents were two of the founding members of Glendale Presbyterian Church. You also know that I am not a stranger to the Episcopal Church, my first wife belonging to Grace Episcopal in Kirkwood, where my son was also baptized. But for me, despite all that, you are the church, its representative, it's front-line.

An envelope, a stamp, a writing pad, a spare pen and phone calls, all requests imposed upon your good office too frequently to readily admit. Your assistance in launching and managing the distribution of What's Up magazine, (along with Vince), lobbying on our behalf and, clearly, on behalf of those whose cause you champion. Each act was significant for two main reasons: you didn't have to and nobody lese could or would. You saw your duty, you heard your call and you took direct action. There are few your like in this world.

I knew early on that you were going to be a good person to be acquainted with. I always like to recall when you asked me if there was anything else I needed and I flippantly rejoined, *"A cool glass of cabernet sauvignon would be nice, thank you."* Your face instantly brightened as you recommended a Kendall-Jackson Reserve, *"It's very good AND affordable!"* That joyful memory of your spontaneity and wit can never be taken away from me.

I've written this letter in a tense that indicates that you're still here with us, because, Carol, you are. In our minds, in our hearts, in our resolve to press forward as you would have us do.

Thanks for being here for me, for everyone, with your special gift for combining competence with the common touch. Skills I'm sure you're utilizing even now as you serve in that Great Company gathered round about the throne of God.

"Till we see you again,

Robert E. Lipscomb, January, 2003

Plundering the Poor

Ω

Okay, I gots me some bones to pick wit ya'll and it goes like this. Now, don't get me wrong, here, I like to stay upbeat about all this stuff but, sometimes, the cold rage inside heats up a bit to where I just have to vent it out or explode in some utterly unacceptable manner. So here goes.

Now, we all know that triage is a standard system in emergency rooms used to deliver care that maximizes the successful survival of the maximum number of victims. Speaking from the old-school military perspective, this means first rendering aid to those injured that will probably survive and recover. Next, the more severely injured and those in need of lots of resources, (always limited,) are treated. Finally, those victims most likely to die are treated, but without throwing away precious resources on folks who are going to die anyway. Makes a certain sense, no? This method results in high recovery rates and prevents the wasting of limited resources, scarcer talent and precious time. I propose to you, good reader, that social service centers would do well to follow the tried and true methodology of medical triage to deliver their services and achieve success in their missions.

Unfortunately, for their client population of homeless and mentally ill, most social service agencies practice the perverted art of reverse triage. How so? Well, for example, a homeless psychotic can find ready sanctuary and counseling services. The louder you are, the more grease you get. But, and here's the real rub, if you are homeless and NOT egregiously mentally ill or addicted to anything, you will not be afforded easy sanctuary nor counseling. You will, instead, be left to fend with the merciless weather and your own demons, on your own.

While every substance-dependent person in the areas sees to their laundry being done, the sober, broke folks are turned away to find other means to meet their daily living needs. Seemingly simple tasks like acquiring fresh clothing or laundering whatever you have, finding suitable shelter, even getting a haircut, become needlessly complicated. If you've been a Boy Scout, you're on your own. Proper behavior is punished while badass cretins are coddled. The hopeless cases who will probably never be "saved", nor recover from their addictions, nor emerge from poverty are using up the very limited resources out there. But, those who, due to personal discipline and adequate social skills could actually benefit from some logistical support and re-enter mainstream society, are utterly ignored.

This is reverse triage. It ain't justice. It defies logic and ignores established, proven methods. It does have one, undeniable result: the perpetuation of a needy class and the employment security of social service professionals. This is evil afoot in the land. To proclaim an organization as existing to help the needy but operating in a fashion that traps and guarantees failure is as satanically inspired as a hospital pouring skills and resources into an attempt to revive someone dead on arrival, while leaving treatable patients to slowly bleed to death in the waiting room.

Once upon a time, this guy named Jesus aka Christ asserted that "the poor are always with you…" Today's gross and self-serving interpretation of this statement is that the poor will always be there no matter what one does and that poverty has no solution. It may be, as I see it, the subtle nuance of Christ's statement that we are to remember NOT that poverty is going to always exist, (how convenient and profitable that would be for many,) but rather that society should SEE the needy among them and not allow the poor to become invisible.

Once seen and comprehended, action is demanded. On this one understanding alone, the entire social services empire could be revolutionized. In the meantime, I have time to pen this little tirade. Time until the Federal government checks are delivered to the "disabled" to fund yet another round of crack and alcohol self-destruction and mayhem. Then, even my quiet little place in this magnificent library will be over-run, once again, by the fully fueled mad-dogs of this city.

Oh, wait. I'm not done just yet…

Oh, how we laughed, we humble souls, perusing an ad in the local newspaper by one of our more-esteemed emergency shelters for the homeless. Every night, night after night, our remnant tribe shuffles woefully, if also gratefully, through the gray, steel door at the shelter, seeking warmth, sustenance, safety, a shower, sleep. Of the forty-four beds, not more than ten are ever occupied by our minority group, that is to say, white men. By far and away, men's shelters in this city are utilized in the vast instance by the African-American poor. I suspect it's like that in most American cities.

Why, then, are the holiday season ads for all of the local shelters using pictures of white men, or a white woman with a blond child? We chuckle because we all know the answer.

We know that potential financial donors are predominately white. In a strongly polarized society, those folks are far less likely to give money to an organization that promotes itself as providing services to blacks, ex-convicts, future convicts, dope fiends, deadbeats and every variety of head case. The shelters do not believe they can depict themselves as they truly are and have any real hope of raising the funds they need to continue operating. The Bottom Line here: *If you want to get big bucks from white folks around here, you got to make them think their donations are going to other white folks.*

One shelter's ad depicts a white male who is, in fact, a model who posed for a New York City ad agency. This guy appears in ads in cities throughout the country or wherever the demographic of potential donors indicates it would be most profitable.

The "mother and daughter" picture in another shelter's ad was lifted from a rural agency's files, not from the urban domain. Point of fact, of all the woman and children camping out around downtown, they are invariably African-American, with only the occasional white gal passing through.

There exists today, therefore, an unsettling legacy of racist mentality coupled with the plundering of the poor, as evidenced by these "white folks need your help" ads. No portrayal of the real homeless population is permitted or useful. About 90% of the donations raised during this holiday season will go to help African-Americans, such funds donated by rich folks desiring to help the kind of people depicted in the shelter's plea ads: *other white folks.*

Make of this whatever you will.

Hold on, I'm not done yet. I gots some more questions raisin' a quandary amongst us po-folks.

Which well respected homeless shelter, with an evangelistic patter, thinks nothing of tossing their homeless occupants out into a pre-dawn blizzard on Christmas Day? All the while proclaiming the mercy of Jesus…

In which shelters will certain staff personnel sell to a shelter guest: a) food, 2) clothing, 3) drugs…And, which shelter can a would-be guest obtain additional housing time for cold cash?

Why did the charity you donate to probably rip you off by stealing your money, goods and services you intended for the poor?

Carloads of good quality clothing come thru the front door of a well-known charity organization, which promises to distribute it all to the needy...*Why*, then, do the same "thrift store" opera-tors drive away regularly with truck loads of those donated items, to be sold?

What famous person pledged a couple million dollars to a local homeless shelter and then couldn't determine how the money was spent?

What well-respected shelter stages deluxe meals for photo-ops and fits beautiful, new colorful blankets on the shelter beds during donor tours? Do you realize that those meals are never served and the blankets are removed after the potential donors leave?

Winter coats gathered at great, annual coat-rallies are unceremoniously dumped in trashbins behind a well-known homeless shelter. To insure that nobody can retrieve and use these coats, cooking grease and motor oil is then poured over the coats, some of which are brand new. *Do you know this is done* because the shelter operator, a nut-job evangelist, believes the new coats may be sold for "crack money", so she would rather a hobo potentially freeze to death and that all hobos must be screwed-up, at least, in this f—k's own, bent mind.

What exactly did the staff at one international organization established to help the poor do with the proceeds of government-issued food stamp cards obtained from homeless clients under their "care"?

What is the real success percentage for home-folks actually obtaining adequate, liveable-wage employment via their St. – Center counselor?

Is the ubiquitous presence and forced avail-ability of spoiled bologna sandwiches Saddam Hussein's diabolical plan to destroy America? Note to the wise: Look for the tell-tale *"Bin Laden Bologna Factory"* label wherever you shop!

Is it probable that Whats Up magazine is just another young liberal's feel-good project that will ultimately end up two-lines of a political resume?!?

Editor's Note: The above was submitted by an independent reporter and does not necessarily reflect the opinions, views or, for that matter, good taste of the publisher. Or anybody else we claim to know. Selah.

*

Legal Aid Goes to War

Ω

The good kids of the local law schools often drop into Christ Church Cathedral's "Club Cathedral" to round up anyone living on the street that has any outstanding warrants, child-support claims, etc. That accounts for a significant percentage of this population. The law students, backed by the real lawyers of the Legal Aid society, try to coax out of the usually recalcitrant client the facts of the concern. It was, then, with certain, natural osmosis that these same lawyers and their righteous young protégés heard about the crisis involving our *Whats Up* magazine vendors and others.

Without pretending to cover all the details of the eventual law suit placed against the City of St. Louis over the reputed actions of some of their police officers, here is the main point. Magazine vendors, allegedly covered by the city-issued permits and operating in a non-obstructive and lawful manner, where being accosted by the police, stripped of their magazines and any few dollars collected, hustled off to three-day stays in jail, charged an un-payable bail or fine amount and, on occasion, even driven to a remote and desolate area of the city, there to be dumped out of the police vehicle, the semi-arrested hoboes on their own to make way to safe harbor.

It was in the environment of this situation that I wrote the following feature for *Whats Up* magazine.

OUR First Amendment tradition is a descendant of 19th century classical liberalism that preached free markets and laissez faire in the economic sphere, maximum individual liberty in the social and political realms and limited government. As a partial result of this tradition, today institutions like mega-media corporations, energy companies, financial institutions, etc. are treated as individuals and accorded the same First Amendment rights as any single mother experiencing homelessness. The difference is, of course, the former's power to dominate public debate. Thus, while proudly waving aloft the free speech banner, we watch our political system being bought out from under us. Effective speech in the current age is not cheap.

The Homeless Grapevine in Cleveland went to court for the right to stay on the street, (peddling newspapers.) In 1994, Cleveland police began ticketing Grapevine vendors, saying they needed to spend $200 in fees and licenses to sell the paper, according to Editor Brian Davis. On September 27, 1994, the American Civil Liberties Union of Ohio sued the city of Cleveland, claiming that *Grapevine* had a First Amendment right to sell on the street. The city lost the case, but later won on appeal. Though the city had long demanded that *Grapevine* vendors be licensed to sell in public, vendors applying for licenses found that, in fact, no such licenses ever existed! Licenses are very specific and the scope of the city's licensing had never covered written matter before, so no such permits could be issued. What followed was months of negotiations about the language and restrictions of the permits, while vendors continued, of course, to be arrested for not having the required permits, permits which never existed! When the licenses were finalized, *Grapevine* vendors, all of whom were struggling to make a precarious living by selling the paper, were asked to pay $50 for each permit. One may as well ask for a million dollars. After all the harassment, ticketing, insulting licensing requirements and a long stint in legal limbo, the ranks of the vendors were cut in half. When asked what former vendors might be doing now instead of peddling the newspaper, Editor Brian Davis replied, *"Probably panhandling again. And, get this, they're not getting ticketed for that!"*

All of that brings us into the a better light of what is happening now inn St. Louis. We at *Whats Up* magazine offer an alternative source of information and entertainment to the established periodicals, such as, the *Post-Dispatch* or the chain-owned *River-front Times*. We concentrate on reporting features about urban social justice and environmental issues and, sometimes, raise the ire of powerful, institution-alized interests. We use a vending model that effec-tively bypasses the entry barriers to distribution that our competitors have erected to secure their own monopolies in the free exchange of ideas and infor-mation. Therein lies the latest rub.

Although each and every one of our vendors who offer copies of our publication to passersby is duly permitted by the City of St. Louis to accept donations on behalf of our state and federally registered non-profit corporation, the police department continues to ignore both our locally granted and our constitutionally protected rights to do so. Dozens of documented incidents involve certain police officers taking it upon themselves to grab stacks of our magazine out of the hands of our permitted vendors and discard or destroy those copies, arrest our vendors on bogus charges of loitering, and so forth, effectively inhibiting our First Amendment rights. The fact that some of these very same police officers even openly brag that it is their intention to stop *Whats Up* magazine from being offered in downtown St. Louis has led us to publicly reveal this on-going, unacceptable situation.

What is most amazing to us here is that dozens of similar cases have already occurred in other cities and the courts have almost uniformly decided that the police are wrong and that non-profit,

157

free press publications may be distributed on the public sidewalks of any city in the United States of America. For it to be otherwise would serve to negate both the letter and intent of the First Amendment to the US Constitution that guarantees each citizen's right to free speech and a free, unfettered press.

Then again, maybe we should shut up and let the police department hang themselves while we rake in big bucks from an ensuing lawsuit...Class action lawsuits have already been awarded millions of dollars in other cities, paid for by those cities' governments. It seems impossible the city's legal counsel is unaware of this.

A parallel situation is also occurring now with the Downtown Community Court being sued in a class-action claiming they are operating an unconstitutional court engaging in selective enforcement of remarkably questionable "quality of life" violations. While the intent is a positive one and any investment or attention to issues involving those experiencing homelessness is welcome, we believe there exists a better model for the four hundred plus individuals so far affected by this court's operations. We are hoping that at some point the city fathers and their police officers will "wise up" and recognize our right to existence and allow us the exercise of our rights. Are these prosecutors and politicians willing to risk all of the above just to thwart our humble publication from being offered? What possible motivation could they have for this attitude given the certain liability they will risk? Some possible answers to this come to mind.

For instance, the police have significant incentives to harass our vendors because our vendors are mostly homeless or under-employed and their presence on the streets is not deemed conducive to a pleasant social environment. And, for sure, some homeless folks are aesthically marginal; so to speak...Yet, bad behavior would be counter-productive to our overall cause, as we desire another ten thousand downtown dwellers move in who can then buy our little magazine.

To those police officers who have respected the rights of our vendors and have demonstrated a willingness to work with our team, as long as the individual vendor does not attempt unlawful behavior, we extend our deep appreciation for your wisdom and sense of fair-play. We must expect, demand really, the same from every police officer, his or her commanders and their civilian superiors, as it is our already existing right to operate fully and freely. Further, it is an insult and disrespect to the City government for police officers to ignore the very permits our vendors carry that have been issued by the City in the first place.

The other main reason we have encountered so much difficulty in distributing our publication, we must surmise, is that a great deal of fear exists in the minds of those opposing us. Perhaps that the content of our magazine is not beholden large advertisers and powerfully entrenched special interest groups? Or, that we continue to accurately and persistently identify, investigate and report on social justice issues, the urban environment and other matters that disturb the comfortable and simultaneously lend comfort to those disturbed by poverty, illness, the class system, and a broken, ineffective judicial system?

It seems to us here at our little outpost of ideas that only fear could motivate the sorts of responses received from the special interests and their strong-arm forces. In this, we naturally take a certain honor and pride. In fact, it is an axiom of social justice that the more entrenched interests persist in their attempted repressions, the stronger the voice of the people becomes.

The arrest and jailing of free press advocates on bogus charges is the hallmark of arrogant, tyrannical, shortsighted government.

We have already made strategic alliance in principle with national organizations and prominent, nationwide publications that stand ready to voice their unified support of our struggle to continue existence here in St. Louis. Two major financial grants have been recently received, one from a major, local commission and the other from a business foundation. What we do here and what we are trying to accomplish has thus received both local and national validation. For any local strong-arm tactic to attempt denial of that validation is to risk their ultimate defeat and real consequences affecting their political, professional and social lives in the St. Louis area. In a city dominated by Democrats, one can only wonder how some have come to resemble totalitarians of dead eras rather than the champions of diversity and fair play they so loudly trumpet each election cycle.

This state of affairs cannot stand. We call on all good people of conscience and American-style fair play to rebuke those who have chosen the way of "might makes right" over our constitutional rights and traditions. We plead that those who have gone astray due to fear re-think their actions in the heart-felt effort to return to their true colors.

As *for Whats Up* magazine and our brave, little band of vendors, we will stay the course in the best traditions of those giants who came before us and whose shining light of freedom guides us unto this day and in the days to come, no matter what. God Bless America.   *Fini.*

The Legal Aid lawsuit against the City was awarded a huge sum of money to be paid out to known victims of police harassment and the rest placed in special funds to be used to enhance the overall wellbeing of the city's most desperate citizens.

We cannot state with certainty that this article had anything to do with that victory, but we prefer to believe it did.

*

The Hope in Things Unseen

Ω

He emerged from the pre-dawn haze, all stealth without furtiveness, intent on avoiding being stoned to death in the minds of passersby. Seeking private space in public places, the quiet doorway, perhaps later some shade, maybe to be blessed with a park bench all to himself. Silence everywhere save within. Accompanied by a mind whose thoughts wave and fold, rise and recede on a never-ceasing tidal flow of memories, some good, most not. Dubious as to whether an event really ever occurred long ago, shadowed, edited for consumption, spun by heavy dollops of wishful thinking, ego defenses, rationalizations, depression-driven denials. Knowing that there is everything to do today and yet nothing to be done about any of it. Resourceless except for a dim, flickering flame of faith that illuminates the hope of things to be better sometime, somehow, somewhere, in some way. Despite all modern reason ruling in opposition, it is that fragile faith that sustains his life.

He is the common, homeless man; by what conceit can he hold such faith? Ah, therein lays the crux of my tale.

For the common hobo, (a self-inflicted sobriquet so sheath your p.c. sabers,) each day arrives promising and playing out much like the previous one, like some evil Hindu Wheel of Life. For homeless me taking fair advantage of the four main shelters in this city, each day's routine also involves, at minimum, a partial helping of preaching each evening. Ranging the gambit from professional to fledgling, these preachers find men in shelters a captive audience usually more eager to be encouraged by a reading of an uplifting Bible passage than the average, normal citizen might suspect. I never heard from a Jewish or Islamic religious preacher while journeying through these shelters, but I do know they often provided food and other resources, in the background.

The Holy Bible is, of course, replete with references designed for and targeted for the relief of sufferings, especially among the poor and powerless.

Robert E. Lipscomb

Beginning in Exodus with chastisements regarding the *"inexcusable mistreatment"* of the poor by the powerful, to the call on the mighty in Deuteronomy to *"abolish poverty,"* culminating in Proverbs which proclaims that *"the Lord God himself defends the poor!"* I read these verses and find hope in the midst of meaninglessness, faith in things I cannot yet see.

In a nation whose wealth easily exceeds the combined treasures of all previous empires in history, the lone man finds himself struggling just to survive, to keep the flame lit, somehow glowing in the dark night of poverty and dismay.

Who says it's all meaningless? I suppose if one is to continue along the original lines of the three peoples of the faith, (Jew, Christian, Muslim,) one can claim that the Great Adversary, Satan if you prefer, started this whole line of thinking that all life is meaningless. And why shouldn't he? After all, if a creature is opposed to the creator of all things, what better way to raise a revolt against that same creator than by proving all creation to be futile, meaningless, absurd? If I believe that my life is absurd and meaningless, I am in opposition to that life's creator. Well, I cannot accept that. That will place me in opposition to God and in communion with the revolution of Lucifer. Is this too simplistic? Have I somehow missed the finer nuances, the hidden metaphors, the tricks of the tale? Or, are all of the above just more ways to distract and divert one simple, shining truth; that God's creations, including this humble life I call mine, are worth something of value, meaningful, not absurd, if for no other reason that it all issues from the will of God. Too circular? Can I argue with myself into a meaningless circle with no decision? Sure. That's possible. In God's creation, all things are possible and that is the point.

Well, if that be so, that all of God's creations are worthwhile because they are creations of God, then isn't that common hobo of some value also?

I write for the joy of witnessing, to present my own testimony. Assorted professionally brilliant folks may cynically refer to this as some kind of Saint Francis Syndrome, my work and words some nutty attempt to save every creature. If you knew the depths of my anger, you would not think this. I am perhaps some Jacobean vagabond priest, some urban monk, finding solace in the scripting, spiritually discharging any lingering debts to my own previous distractions and delusions, my sin of existence.

"Better righteous poverty than tainted wealth...Poverty is better than dishonesty!" proclaims David in his Psalms. Here, I find the common hobo may possess a higher moral caliber than society's icons of wealth and popularity. I've been successful; how I wish to tell them what you hold in your hands is not the world but a fragile, hollow globe of illusions.

It is the spirit-filled action that sustains the pride and dignity of our poorest and most disadvantaged. Are we poorer than those whose wealth lies in the deceit of riches when ours resides in the "true wealth" described in Revelations? How disadvantaged can one be if one's strength and power are founded on the will and hand of a loving creator? Poverty provides a divine opportunity as promised in Proverbs 19 and again in Mathew 25. Look it up. Thank me later.

It's even more foundationally realized, this thing called faith that I see so wondrously evidenced among society's shuffling wraiths. Often closer to death than to life, the hobo may be closer to God than your average citizen. Have I not glimpsed the narrow-boned soul, seeming otherworldly as if a ghost re-materializing, becoming bodily spirit, enabled, soulful? The slim chance for justice may be carried on those slim forms.

The homeless man may find fresh bond with God in his financial and familial crisis and in the latter's existence in a culture polluted beyond recognition by the determined worship of each deadly sin. Both God and the poor man find abandonment their fate, thus forging an alliance of kindred beings unique to them.

The hobo enters the light of each new day, strumming the seven strings of the covenant in his heart, reminded constantly of the sins he must depart from and of the covenant with his king.

Becoming homeless after experiencing a half-century of "normalcy" is akin to a reverse metamorphosis, wherein the once-beautiful butterfly becomes the nondescript caterpillar. But, as any school child will tell you, with the warming sun of God's love and a few good friends, someday, maybe someday soon, the caterpillar will emerge to the world again as the beautiful butterfly and soar free.

This is the hope in things unseen.

This is the faith of the homeless man.

Selah.

*

Candlemass

Ω

I have reached the vanishing point of my so-journ upon the streets. I have learned what I came here to learn, now things merely repeat and I have no further time for it.

There is one place that has come to be my home, where I always feel welcome and protected. I fear it a cliché but, in truth, I don't really care how others judge it. My sanctuary is a sanctuary, of the Cathedral variety. My family is here, those who grant me love and patience and certain levels of compre-hension. Today we celebrate the day Christ entered the temple as a child and debated with the priests there.

I enter the Cathedral called Christ Church Episcopal and find a seat. It wasn't always so. This has been a long time coming. For months, years really, I could not bring myself to declare another church, to say to Glendale Presbyterian Church that I am done with you. You are eternally in my heart of hearts, you are my other home, but time and circumstance has called me elsewhere and it is there I must address the priests, state my intentions, teach and learn and teach and learn. It is here, near my gallant, lost legion of concrete-commandoes, that I will stay.

And, yes, there is that immanent affair of faith blossoming with my dear friend Sharon. I have loved other women before and they were good women at the time. Through trial and error, mostly the latter, I have come to this place with Sharon in my mind and heart. I believe if I sit still she will know to find me here. The street-life for me is over. I cannot return to any shelter, would rather sleep with a blanket of snow on me, somewhere dark and strong, some- where in this great city.

I see three or four street folks enter the Cathe- dral sanctuary. I reach for my wallet and extract four one dollar bills, two paper bus tickets and a lottery ticket that hit for two dollars prize. I give them away to the cadre before me. I don't need these tokens that are such a blessing to those here who do. I pull out my pay-as-you- go cell phone and dial Sharon's number, get her voicemail, tell her where I am and of my decision. My prepaid time runs out near the end of my message. It is a symbol to me of my time on these streets having run out. Go to the temple, they told Mary. There you will find the one you seek.

It is getting late and the maintenance crew wants to close and lock the sanctuary, shooing everyone out. Jim McGahey pauses in front of me, seeming to make a decision whether or not to ask me to leave. He says quietly, *"You can stay here as long as you need to. Just let me know when you're leaving so I can lock up the building and go home."*

Jim is a secret hero of mine. It is he who caught Carol Bledsoe, the murdered church secretary, as she fell mortally wounded to the floor in the hallway of the Bishop Tuttle Memorial building. It was Jim who was with her in her final moments on earth. He is a hero. I resolve to tell him I think so, maybe later, sometime.

An exasperated Sharon comes huffing into the Cathedral sanctuary. *"There you are!"* she exclaims.

Where did you think I'd be? I ask softly.

Will you come home with me, end this journey now? She asks, some fear in her voice.

Yes, I reply. *I will go with you. It is time to go home.*

*

A Chat with Lee Stringer

Ω

Lee Stringer is the author of the bestseller "Grand Central Winter", a book he wrote while homeless, drug addicted and writing, on occasion, for a street newspaper. I originally met Lee at a NASNA conference in Boston and more recently had the opportunity to hear him speak to the Transitional Program's writing workshop provided by Peter & Paul Men men's shelter in the Soulard. (That's right, the same place I first landed when I hit the streets.) We chatted later, also, after his book signing at the wonderful bookstore Left Bank Books in the St. Louis Central West End. The following is derived from those separate conversations with this intriguing author. For simplicity of editing and conservation of page space, the WU below is me on behalf of Whats Up magazine.

WU: Welcome to St. Louis, Lee, it's a real pleasure to see you again. I've been intrigued by your success since learning about you at the NASNA conference in Boston a couple of years ago. Can you tell us a little something about how you managed to write you first book while living in such difficult circumstances?

Lee: Much like you, Bob, I got interested in writing after hooking up with the street magazine in New York City, called *"Street News."* I had a musty composition book that I just started writing in, scrawling really, and then found I was into it. Really into it.

WU: It takes some clarity of thinking to produce a credible work for others to read. Can you describe for us what your own situation was then, what factors negative or positive you had to cope with?

Lee: Half the time, I was bombed out on drugs or alcohol. I was living in a tunnel under New York City's Grand Central Terminal. The word "terminal" had a dual meaning. Much of what I wrote was just gibberish, rubbish. But, sifting through the heap of scratchings, some things of value began to emerge. Others, mostly the staff at a drug rehab clinic I was in and out of at the time, began to comment on my writing. It was both unsettling and intriguing. I suppose the positive attention I got from my writing efforts encouraged me to continue, even if a lot of it was junk.

WU: Sounds like a lesson in there. I think I understand that experience. To keep honing the craft until something of value emerges.

Lee: Definitely. Don't give up. Volume will necessitate more and more use of your brain. Keep those brain cells firing. Also, the more you write, the less time one might devote to less productive activities, shall we say.

WU: Like getting high or drunk or mixed up in street brawling and all the other bad things that can happen when you're living on the street?

Lee: Exactly. Re-focus is everything. Also, getting your mother to let you crash at her place and pound out your musing on an ancient computer. Most moms won't let you in the door if they suspect you're gonna act up.

WU: Your first book, *"Grand Central Winter"*, was a compilation of short stories from your life. Nothing especially dramatic or unique. Yet, the skill of your story-telling resonated with your readers and the book became a bestseller. What's the lesson there?

Lee: You're right. My tale is just one of ten million stories in the Big Apple. Any skill I may have can best be summed up in this: *Keep it real.* Authenticity counts. The reality of your story must be perceived by the reader, understood, grasped. This is not always an easy thing, but most readers are amazingly perceptive and will detect a bullshit artist quick like. There's a lot of bullshit out there in print right now. My advice is that if you can keep it real, heartfelt and convey that in your writing, you'll achieve some level of success. Also, (laughing,) it helps to be in the publishing capital of the world, (New York City.)

WU: I think everybody here tonight, (at Lee's reading of excerpts from his books,) was touched by your genuineness, your humanity. Perhaps that is what makes your books so well accepted.

Lee: That's kind of you to say. I'd like to think that's true, 'cause I'm gonna be me, can't help it, so everything I write from here on out is in some way going to reflect this writer.

WU: Thank you, Mr. Stringer. Thank you for your inspiration, your heart, your work.

Lee: Thanks, Bob. And, best of luck on your first book!

WU: Thank you. You know I will probably be calling for you for a jacket blurb.

Lee: (chuckling) Anytime, Bob, anytime.

The end.

The beginning.

*

Robert E. Lipscomb

Coming soon!

"Just Beyond

Down Town"

The story continues with new adventures,

sudden tragedies, inspiring triumphs!

Available early 2007

Coming soon!

"An Affair of Faith"

Available Spring, 2007

Robert E. Lipscomb

Coming Soon!

"City of God"

A novel of power and pride, tragedy and triumph at the turn of the 20th century

2003 NASNA Award winner

ROBERT E. LIPSCOMB

Available Spring, 2007

For the latest titles from and information
about Eagle's View Press, LLC., St. Louis, just
visit us at: www.eaglesviewpress.com
Author's website: www.robertelipscomb.info

For bulk order discounts or Special Editions
for associations and corporations, inquire:
info@eaglesviewpress.com
*(Special Editions may be created on a custom-
ized basis including corporate or association
logos and personalized Forward page with
black& white photograph of principle officers.)*

‡

Robert E. Lipscomb